Bounce!

---

101 ESSENTIAL LIFE LESSONS

Kenneth A. Reiss

I

Bounce! 101 Essential Life Lessons
Copyright © 2020 by Kenneth A. Reiss

Published in the United States

Kenneth A. Reiss
Blinker Click Publishing
P.O. Box 9468
Bolton, Connecticut 06043
www.BounceLifeLessons.com

Publisher's Note: This is a combined work of non-fiction and fiction. Names, characters, places, and incidents in the fiction portions are a product of the author's imagination. Locales and public names are sometimes used for atmospheric purposes. Any resemblance to actual people, living or dead, or to businesses, companies, events, institutions, or locales is completely coincidental.

First Edition (Revision C) Published June 2020.

Acknowledgements

I would like to especially thank Catherine Reiss, my wife, Dorothy Reiss, my mother, and Russell Reiss, my father, who stayed committed, positive, and encouraging by my side through this entire life-changing event. Not only did they give me unconditional love, but they kept me motivated to keep going on this book. They reassured me that there were people who needed to read what I was writing, whose lives could be touched and helped by my words. They inspired me to push on when I questioned my ability to make a difference, and they spent tireless hours reading my drafts and giving corrections, improvements, and suggestions. I am deeply grateful for them. This book would not exist without them.

There are an incredible number of other people who have shaped my life and been there for me in ways I often felt I didn't even deserve. I'm sorry I can't list everyone here, but in addition to the joy my children bring me, I'd like to hereby especially thank the following people for having given me so much during this event and the writing of this book: Peter Loening, Timothy Mooney, Karyn Dillon, Jenny Tran, Peter Delaney, Paul D'Addabbo, Mark & Heather Reiss, Rich & Renee Santos, Moo Yong Lee, Lillian Reiss, Thomas Bristovish, Arthur Reiss, Ken Coscia, Nyana, Abraham, Scott Moore, Joan McLaughlin, Jayson Hernandez, Ramone Reynolds, Timothy Searles, Joel Waldron, Allenston Sheridan, Thomas Mockalis, Larry Locks, Beverly Lewis, Cil Padgett, Wayne Bollinger, Kayleigh Cockerill, TJ Benoit, Jennifer Bell, Carrie Hahn, Scott Liscomb, Wayne Morgansen, Mary Robbins, and Eclipse CT.

CONTENTS

adjust to ensure you're still on-course.

never understand.

LET'S GET STARTED...

A Bump. That's all this was... A Speed Bump.

It just slowed me down. It wasn't a big deal. In fact, it helped me. But at the time, it certainly did not feel like help. In fact, it felt like death itself, with all of the same elements: Terror, denial, guilt, anger, sadness, and a quest for understanding. I didn't just move through these elements, as though they were stages. I lived with many of them and, at times, even most of them at the same time. But I got through.

I didn't just survive. Through this enormous event, I struggled, learned and grew.

I struggled with trying to find reason for something I couldn't ever understand. I struggled with accepting a reality that I was helpless to directly change. I struggled with my own mind, who kept telling me "You should have...", "If only you had...", "Why didn't you...", and "You deserve this..."

The lessons I share with you in this book were often snuck into my experience in ways that, only in retrospect, I could see I was learning them. They weren't clearly defined or organized like a school lesson plan. Instead, they always seemed just below the surface, until I actively listened for and eventually received them.

At times, it even seems that my growth was being taught to me by some intelligence much greater than my own. But I guess that's how life works - that intuitive sense which saved a life, that spark of insight that created a masterpiece performance in minutes, or that coincidence where you called someone who had just that moment been thinking of you.

This is a positive book, which came out of a negative experience. My goal was to share with you my numerous lessons, with my *most sincere desire* to help you not only survive any such ordeal yourself, but hopefully to avoid one altogether. I intend on re-reading it every year, for the rest of my life, and to strongly encourage my children and everyone I love to do the same!

"Bump" was the original name of this book. But just as I was finishing it, I changed its name to "Bounce!" Bounce is a much more accurate description of what happened because now that I'm "up" again, I'm higher than I was before this crazy twist of events nearly sunk me and the business I had spent most of my waking hours building for the past 21 years!

This is not just a business book, but instead it is truly a *life book* based on a business event which had many life factors and repercussions. Its lessons are applicable to *anything* you may face in your life! Its lessons are not the standard common life lessons we all have heard before. Instead, they are either entirely new lessons altogether or new adaptations of "common sense."

I've written the events that occurred chronologically, as this helps it all make sense by giving you a timeline and perspective. I've called out the lessons learned at each point, starting with the first one now...

LESSON 1: KICKING YOURSELF WHILE YOU'RE DOWN WON'T GET YOU BACK UP.

L ooking back, I can see numerous places where I would have made different decisions with the knowledge I now have. But at the time, I made the best decisions I could, with the best information and experience I had. In fact, this concept led me to my first lesson, because when I was down, I often added even more negative to my situation by blaming myself for everything.

This seems like an obvious lesson, as many of them may. But that is because only with distance from the challenge, could I see the positive side of the contrast it was offering. When I was drowning in it, I hardly could even breathe... Literally!

LESSON 2: YOU INSIDIOUSLY BECOME COUNTER-PRODUCTIVE WHEN YOU PUSH YOURSELF OUT OF BALANCE.

Maybe it was my nature, upbringing, or life experiences, which led me to fault myself for everything that ever went wrong. But, in the past, I just always worked more hours, tried harder, and put "my nose to the grindstone" and got results. I see now that these were only temporary, off-balance results. I was missing that fact that by saying "yes" to all that extra work, I was inadvertently saying "no" to so much more that was many times even more important.

I was caught in the success trap. You never want to go backwards - it's sort of the major sin of business. I recall in one of my early management jobs, I was taught that all businesses are "either growing or failing." With that mentality, I had to do whatever it took to grow. What a price I paid. I had no idea. I was naive and blind. And, again, at the time, I thought I was doing the right things, especially because apparent success kept coming my way.

LESSON 3: IF YOU DON'T KNOW WHAT MATTERS MOST, NOTHING YOU DO REALLY MATTERS AT ALL.

I'm not saying not to take responsibility for your life or even for your mistakes. But, this responsibility must include a much larger picture of those things which are truly the most precious and valuable to you.

Our culture rewards the extrovert, type-A, go-getter approach. Of course, this is true because you can't just sit in your living room and hope for one million dollars to drop into your lap. But, an introspective, balanced approach will allow us to remain in harmony in such a way that we are truly focusing upon and moving toward that which matters *most* to us!

Even this is a self-fulfilling trap, though, because the more out-of-harmony we become, the less time

KENNETH A. REISS

we spend probing ourselves for that which truly is most important. In addition, our own viewpoint becomes distorted in such a way, that we might even become unable to accurately sense and know that which our inner-self holds most dear. Finally, when we're out of balance we believe more than ever that everything we're thinking is true, right, and correct, which is entirely deceiving. The rush for success and the race for accomplishment become their own values.

Usually later in life than sooner, we all eventually see clearly, and many of us have no more time left to do anything about it. In this regard, I am so incredibly blessed to have gone through the ordeal this book is written about, while I am in my mid-life. It helped me clarify and truly *know* my own inner values in ways which would not have been possible with continued success.

The Business

This book is regarding an e-commerce business I started in 2008 out of my front porch. I started with twelve products and by 2013, I had built an online catalog of over 1000 different products! As the daily orders became too much to handle, I leveraged a fulfillment provider, to whom we would ship our products in bulk, which they would then send out to our individual customers. In addition, we found that using a marketplace facilitator for attracting customers, processing payments, and providing first-level customer service, gave us an advantage over just using our own websites.

LESSON 4: WHEN TIMES ARE GOOD, TAKE ADVANTAGE OF OPPORTUNITIES THAT ONLY COME WHEN TIMES ARE GOOD.

Then in 2016, I purchased my partner's half of the business. In order to do this, I took on debt. It was reasonable to do so, as I expected the business' revenue to surpass the monthly debt service and therefore reasonably expected to have it paid off in approximately ten years. Unfortunately, I took it from multiple sources, one of which (the largest one) had only a one-year repayment structure. This forced me to continue to refinance that loan repeatedly, which was costly and ate up cash flow.

Looking back, I learned that I should have refinanced all the debt at that time with some sort of a low-interest, long-term loan, perhaps SBA. But I was so confident of my future success, based on my past success, that I truly believed with every fiber of myself that it would continue!

LESSON 5: EVENTUALLY, THE CYCLE WHICH BROUGHT YOU UP WILL BRING YOU DOWN, IF YOU DON'T CHANGE.

All life is cycles. Time is made of days and years, with their own nights and winters. Space is made of ups and downs, lefts and rights, forwards and backwards. There are even intangible cycles such as good and bad, happy and sad, and right and wrong.

None of these are absolutes - they are always a blend of that which we see as opposites. However, one often becomes dominant. As humans, we like to see the dominant one as reality and the other as nonexistent, at least at that time. But the truth is all points of every cycle are actually still existent and should be recognized as such, in order to retain balance with life.

This isn't to say you can't continue to grow and advance indefinitely. But without identifying, clearly understanding, and adjusting to these cycles, you will become prey of the cycle. *Everything* works in cycles. Understanding and accepting this will allow you to use one cycle as your catalyst for the next one.

It's like the old adage: "Buy low, sell high". But somehow, my mistake was thinking I could enjoy continued success by buying low and waiting forever. This is critically untrue. I had to learn to first accept that letting go is essential and only in doing so could I see clearly. In fact, I think this is one of these lessons which is still being taught to me, even today!

LESSON 6:
LETTING GO IS
ESSENTIAL FOR
THRIVING.

L ater in 2016, I also stocked up heavily, really, really heavily, on inventory for our lucrative holiday season, because the nature of e-commerce is to produce 50% of your annual sales in November & December, and 90% of your profits in the same time period.

To do this I also took on substantial debt. The majority of this debt was also short-term and the rest was on my personal credit cards. I literally 'max'ed everything out. It made sense at the time, to take advantage of the holiday selling season as much as possible.

But, that year, sales declined significantly from past holiday seasons due to inflation, competition, and vendor restructuring. Even though we were doing everything that had worked in the past, we couldn't increase the sales and I ended up with lots of overstock products. This left me with the option of holding on to it, which meant storage and handling costs or clearance-pricing it to generate cash. I decided to do both, depending on how desperately we needed cash flow.

Our world wants to hold on to everything. We keep everything stored, packed, and organized. We even hold on to old emotions, life stories, fears, pains, and regrets. We somehow have come to believe that forever is tangible... That we will be here forever for all this stuff we're holding on to. We won't! We are all dying, one day at a time.

If we hold on to everything, we not only lose our focus on any specific thing and end up only seeing that which we most recently held on to, but we miss the opportunity to see and jump onto the next cycle.

If I had let go of the concept that all our year's profit came in the Holiday Season, I would have seen something happening which I couldn't before: There was a much larger cycle changing right in front of me - I just couldn't see it.

LESSON 7: YOU CAN'T FIX A PROBLEM UNLESS YOU KNOW IT IS A PROBLEM.

In early 2017, I hired an executive to develop and fortify our vendor relations, as a direct response from our declined sales. He did a nice job, but we quickly found that the industry was going through gigantic trends where the manufacturers were confused and struggling with how to balance their brick-and-mortar image vs. their online image. Many of them worked with us and continue to do so, creating a profitable business relationship! However many others decided to try other approaches, such as selling directly themselves, using specialty marketing/distribution services, or limiting their online vendors to just a handful.

As a result, we ended up having over 60% of our product line, 20,000 SKUs, ripped out of our hands over the course of six months. These were products that we had invested significantly into in order to properly satisfy our customers' needs, which included effective marketing, product preparation, intelligent pricing, and even supply flow innovations. It was really disheartening to be told "Effective immediately, you are no longer allowed to sell our products on these marketplace facilitator websites," when *we built their brands* on those platforms!

Had I correctly assessed the handful of vendors, who had done this in the previous years, as a significant trend, I could have made reasonable changes back then, when I had the profitability which would have allowed me the space and time to change. Instead, I saw them as anomalies and tried harder to hold on to those we had.

LESSON 8: IF YOU FIGHT THE TRUTH, THE TRUTH WILL WIN.

I didn't know we had a vendor problem, because I denied what was in front of me. I fought the truth and the truth won. I didn't "go with it" - I resisted what I was seeing, that which was right in front of my eyes, for all of the reasons cited in the previous lessons.

I wasn't actively fighting, though. I was just denying it because each vendor we lost was so painful, both emotionally and financially, that I was just trying to keep up by pouring more energy, time, and money into those that we had, only to eventually lose many of them, too. I can see clearly that all my efforts would have been much better spent on the next cycle.

That which got me the success I was enjoying was NOT going to get me the future successes I needed. There was another cycle, which I wasn't actively looking for, because I was so busy trying to hold on to the old one. The truth was that the old cycle was on the decline and, by ignoring this, perhaps out of optimism or fear, I ended up losing my fight with the truth.

LESSON 9: CUTTING CORNERS NEVER WORKS.

S o, after taking on even more debt to retain our executive's employment and also add more inventory again, although much more conservatively (I learned that lesson!), for the 2017 Holiday Season, I was hit with another surprise.

Five years earlier, I had asked my lawyer to ensure we were sales-tax compliant, which we were. I had written on my recurring, annual to-do checklist, to contact the lawyers again to double check. But I thought I would save some money, because lawyers are not cheap, by skipping this. I thought to myself, "What could have changed? I'm doing the same thing I was before." Little did I know, there was yet another cycle occurring, of which I had absolutely no awareness.

It turns out that there was new sales tax case law, meaning not actual laws, but rules we need to follow based on others who challenged laws. As such, we ended up realizing that we had to become sales-tax compliant in all 50 states overnight. Our inventory was automatically being moved into 39 of these states by our fulfillment provider in order to deliver orders more quickly to our customers. There weren't any laws saying that we had to collect and remit sales tax in all those states, simply because our inventory was there, but there was a court case where a state successfully sued a seller for exactly this.

It cost us severely to address that issue with our lawyers and ensure that we are completely compliant in all 50 states, which even included setting up corporate locations in 39 of them!

By this time, I had no money. My personal net worth had gone very negative, since I was now the sole owner of the business. So, I borrowed again. Amazingly and thankfully, I was blessed with wonderful lenders that were willing to help me through!

So, in 2018, after learning these lessons, I overhauled our inventory management systems to ensure we were bringing in only the best products with the highest profit potential. After all, having so much left over inventory from 2016 (which we still had at that time), caused me to often have to sell products to our customers at prices *below* that which we paid for it initially. That doesn't even take into account years of storage fees we had paid on these items we were selling below our cost! In 2018, this created another large loss, which, again, I somehow miraculously was

KENNETH A. REISS

able to borrow, in order to pay.

In 2019, having had a successful prior year, intentionally eliminating 10,000s of products and adding 10,000s of highly-selective new ones, we were poised for success yet again! Our executive had to leave us for personal reasons, which ended up working out alright for us too (I learned my lesson about not "fighting the truth"). Our team got focused and lean! The inventory mix was perfect! We were starting to pay down debt and had a couple of profitable months, even! All signs showed a bright future.

Then, on October 25, 2019 (Day 1), our selling account was suspended on our largest marketplace facilitator, the one where 99% of our income sourced! This cost us as much *each day* in income as we paid monthly for rent, with all our same expenses which already had been consuming every penny of income!

We had received notices a few weeks prior claiming that we had violated someone else's intellectual property, which we immediately addressed. It turns out that the marketplace facilitator had been so backed up dealing with these that they hadn't even seen our responses to these claims, which included formal retractions by the claimants!

So, they just switched us off, like a light switch, right at the beginning of our Holiday Season! I had just completed re-borrowing every penny of debt I had paid back for the year, in order to have enough inventory for successful holiday sales. By this time, our *daily* debt repayment was as much as our monthly rent and interest was accruing *every month*! So, this holiday season was to be our savior, which I am certain it would have been because we had the right product mix!

So we called and called and called them, only to be told mixed responses, several of which even contradicted each other. Apparently the only way to be reactivated was to admit guilt in writing that we had violated another's intellectual property, which went against my every fiber. But my back was to the wall and I had no other options. So we submitted an appeal indicating as such, fully expecting to be reactivated within 24 hours.

Then, day after day and week after week went by waiting for a response from them. Finally, when we got one, it was that our account had been deactivated again for having too large of a sales discrepancy compared to our history. Of course we did! Our account was turned off by them, so zero sales is 100% less than what it was before!! So, I wrote a response to this effect and received a reply three days later that I hadn't addressed the initial issue.

So, I wrote another reply with even more details and explanation, over 300 pages of documentation, and was then told to just wait for their reply. When we called, we were told to stop calling and that our calls were causing our case to be moved to the "bottom of the list!" So, we stopped calling and waited days, weeks, and months more.

Eventually everything worked out ok, but the remainder of this book is about the daily and hourly struggle I was thrust into and how I survived and what I learned. I most sincerely hope it is helpful to you!

By the way, that last paragraph was a lie: We're not turned on yet. Why lie? Well, I thought that maybe if I wrote it here, I could "speak" it into existence and it would happen but it didn't... yet!!

LESSON 10: BELIEF IN YOURSELF IS ESSENTIAL FOR SUCCESS.

B ut I suspect having written it for you to read and for me to read, shows a type of courage and confidence which is essential to all success. Shows who? The universe? God? My inner-self/soul? Or just "me", that which I call myself? Guess it doesn't really matter.

I have seen over and over in life that believing in yourself will *always* produce better results than not. The mind is a success-seeking mechanism. It moves you toward a desired outcome. You program it with your thoughts.

Ever notice when there is a specific car you're interested in - maybe a new one that just came out, one you want to buy soon, or one a friend just bought - you begin noticing them everywhere? Like magic, it seems the Universe dropped dozens of this type of car in front of you to see, simply because your attention is on it. Is this what happened? Of course not - the cars were there already (see a later section regarding the Infini-verse concept, about whether the cars were *really* there or not) but your subconscious mind caused you to notice them, when you otherwise wouldn't. You see hundreds, maybe thousands of cars each day and 99.999% seem unimportant. But when you're focused on (believing in) something specific, your subconscious calls that out to you.

This is why believing in yourself is critical. When your subconscious believes (actually sees, literally, because it processes all concepts as images) that your success is assured, it will show you opportunities which you would have certainly missed before. It is like magic!

Day 1

At 11:30 AM on Friday, October 25, 2019, we were turned off by our marketplace facilitator. Literally, our sales went to zero! To make matters worse, we were also notified that both the proceeds from previous sales, which were awaiting transfer to our bank account, as well as *all* of our inventory, which we had worked so hard for the past nine months to procure and ship to them, were being *frozen*.

LESSON 11: DON'T BELIEVE EVERYTHING YOU'RE TOLD.

I suppose this should have been an obvious lesson, but apparently I needed to learn it again, perhaps for the 50th or 100th time in my life. I am a very trusting person. I treat everyone how I would like to be treated. I tell them the truth and expect they will tell me the truth. This was a big mistake in this situation.

We immediately called the marketplace facilitator and were told that we just needed to submit an appeal and we would be reactivated shortly. When we asked what "shortly" meant, they said typically a few hours or a few days at most. Wow, was this a lie! Now, perhaps the agents we spoke with truly didn't know what to say, but this *is* their job.

So, we drafted an appeal letter explaining that the intellectual properly complaints we received from these Chinese companies had been retracted by them. In addition, we agreed to improve our systems for overseeing future item listings.

Here's how all this works. One seller on the marketplace, let's say business A, initially lists a product for sale. They create the initial listing. Then let's say sellers B, C, and D also sell the same product on the same listing, but have slightly different information in their listing. This is very common as additional sellers may include more details to help the customer or which the first seller didn't have or choose to omit initially.

But what happens when the information is directly contradictory to the initial information? Well, the marketplace facilitator then has to use their algorithms to figure out which information to show. It is unclear how they do this, and they even have a whole process for reporting incorrect decisions, so a human in their organization can try to figure out what changed.

However, in some cases, we strongly suspect that one of the new sellers tries to "hijack" the listing. Effectively, they try to steal it by changing the Brand Name of the item to their own. Once they succeed at doing this, they then can initiate intellectual property claims against all the other (legitimate) sellers. This is exactly what happened to us.

When we first listed on these items, we were 100% certain that the listings showed the exact brands we were selling. In fact, we would never list it any other way, out of fear of violating any laws or disappointing our customers. We train all our employees to respect our customers at the highest level! Our customers, after all, are the boss of *all of us*!

So, back in early October when we received these two initial intellectual property claims, we thought nothing of it. We get five to ten such complaints each year and regularly and immediately address them. In most cases we just end up having our inventory on that product sent back to us (at our expense) and discontinue selling on the listing to avoid any potential conflict. In this case, too, we closed the listings and didn't even have any inventory to send back! We weren't even selling the products!

We explained this to the two claimants, who immediately retracted their claims. However, apparently, the marketplace facilitator, for an unknown reason, did not address these promptly, as they always had in the past. Instead, they took so many weeks that their time-frame to address the issue passed and our account was suspended.

We truly believed we would be back on later that day or the next, and certainly by Monday at the absolute latest. We called them five more times that day and were told that the case was there and that it would be reviewed when they got to it.

During this time, we continued to ship product to them. In fact, over the next few weeks, we sent another 25% more inventory to them to be prepared and ready for the upcoming busy holiday season. If

I had known we would be turned off for *months* instead of hours, I never would have done this. I would have saved the cash, to pay the bills for the following months!

LESSON 12: ALWAYS SAVE FOR THE RAINY DAY, BECAUSE THE RAINY DAY WILL COME.

B eing an incredibly optimistic person and having had many sales over the past eleven years, I had no reason to expect we wouldn't be turned on again promptly, certainly before the holiday season really started. Nothing like this had ever happened to us... ever!

As such, I continued to spend with confidence on additional inventory for the holiday season. Our awesome team worked long, hard hours getting everything shipped out to the fulfillment centers. Of course, this entire inventory was purchased on credit, either bank lines of credit, credit cards, or vendor credit.

Had I learned this lesson prior to October 25, I

would have put money or more aside, just in case. Luckily, I did slow my buying a bit over the coming weeks, and when the fulfillment centers finally stopped taking our orders, I halted immediately.

Never think a rainy day won't come. It will, and often without warning. It's not like there was a weather forecast I could have tuned in to, to prepare for this. Or was there?

LESSON 13: LISTEN TO AND HEED THE ADVICE OF KNOWLEDGEABLE PEOPLE YOU TRUST WHO ADVISE YOU.

As I look back, I can clearly see three people who tried to warn me about this. All three of them had decades more experience in both business and life than I did, and they all really cared about me. Their intent was only purely to be helpful.

The first was my martial arts (Taekwondo) teacher. He passed away three years prior, but we went to an event where people ask dead people questions and get responses. I know... it sounds strange, but we tried it! While my teacher didn't "talk" to me there, it all seemed so believable and legitimate, that we took the phone number of the people running the event and scheduled a phone consultation. This was actually for my wife, but my teacher "came through" on her call and had clear messages for me, including one that said I need to look at the details which are right in front of me. If I don't, there could be significant financial trouble.

The second was my father. With decades starting, building, and operating a highly successful business, he had just two weeks prior told me to be careful when working with big companies like the marketplace facilitator we were using. He warned me that they can be fickle and often have motives that small businesses owners like me couldn't understand. He encouraged me to be careful and have alternatives in place.

The third was my real estate advisor, who has become a close, trusted business friend. Just a week prior, I met with him regarding some financial planning to try to get out of debt appropriately. He warned me that one of the largest risks he saw in me consolidating my debt was that all my eggs were in this one basket.

I didn't listen to all three of them! I thought I knew better. I thought that I somehow I deserved success and that the marketplace facilitator wouldn't do something like this to me. I didn't set my ego aside and listen... truly *listen* to what they told me, from their amazing experience. It wasn't that I didn't hear them, but instead was that I didn't *want* to hear them! Somehow, I thought I could sail through without issue.

After all, I had just come through five years of excruciating times, wondering each month if we were going to stay in business or not. I could finally see some light at the end of the tunnel and I was so excited that I didn't want anyone to rain on my parade. Silly me! If I could have seen that listening and heeding their advice would have saved me innumerable amounts of grief in the coming months, I would have gladly done so. But hindsight is 20/20!

LESSON 14: DON'T BLAME OTHERS FOR YOUR FAILURES.

This was my failure. I was the sole business owner. I was going to enjoy all the financial success, when it finally came. I was the one dealing with it.

But at the time, I hadn't yet learned this lesson and quite strongly blamed my wife, who was also the company employee who handled all concerns of this nature. I couldn't believe she had let this happen. How could she have not followed up sooner on those claims from early October? How could she have not paid attention to deadlines, etc?

She was devastated. She loves me immensely, and *never ever, ever* would have done anything to hurt me or our family. She was raising our 20-month old son and had just given birth to our six-week old daughter. She was completely overcome with guilt and grief over the situation.

I treated her horribly. Not just implying that this

was her fault, but actually telling her this. This was entirely unjustified and was very, very little of me to do. This lesson took me days to learn.

I immediately saw how much I had hurt her and tried hard to help her recover. But, internally, it took me ten more days, inside my mind, before I stopped blaming her. What a horrible thing for me to have done!! I felt enormous guilt and pain for having hurt her so deeply. Luckily, I was able to learn from it and take responsibility, which really meant not blaming her for this. And, somehow, my incredible wife still loved me and even forgave me for my hurtful, wrong behavior!

Day 3

By the time Sunday came, my blame had extended far beyond my wife. I was blaming the marketplace facilitator, too. After all, they were the ones who shut us off. But in reality, they were just following their policies. These were policies I had readily agreed to evelen years ago when I signed their contracts.

I started blaming everyone else, too, including strangers and people who had nothing to do with this! Luckily I kept my mouth closed most of the time and eventually came to see clearly that the *only person with blame was myself!* Somehow blaming them seemed to make this less real and more tolerable, at least in my mind.

I know it was a horrible thing to do, which is why I am sharing it with you. I never would have done that under normal circumstances, but in this chaos, my mind was looking for relief and found it in blaming others.

I have since learned that I should have been checking these types of claims more often. I should have monitored better. I should have spot-checked the product listings. I should have even written software which would have pulled the current brand name for our entire catalog of 25,000 products and compared them to the brand name we knew it to be, so we could take appropriate action on those which had been hijacked to entirely avoid such a crisis as this. (By the way, at the time of this publication, I have written this software and it is working magnificently!)

But, by day 3, I was really getting frustrated! I kept multiplying the number of days we were turned off by the daily lost sales, and that total was now really adding up! It was a LOT of money... more than we make in profit in an entire month! More than four months of my home mortgage!! And somehow I still had to pay the bills with borrowed money and somehow make up this loss, from a position of extreme debt. It seemed impossible!!

LESSON 15: THROUGH CONTRAST WE GAIN CLARITY AND LEARN ABOUT OURSELVES.

B
ut I was able to step out of the situation, in my mind, and try to see a much bigger picture. I realized that, long-term, I didn't ever want to be in this situation again. I never wanted to be "owned" or "trapped" by the actions of some third-party. I vowed to myself that when this is over, I will take steps to ensure nothing like this can ever happen again. I will put in place safeguards, both in the form of financial reserves as well as diversification, so that I will never allow myself to be in this position again. But somehow I had to get turned back on and then dig out of this mountain of debt, too.

Day 4

By Monday, I fully expected to be turned back on. There was no doubt in my mind! When we weren't I was somehow able to remain very confident and calm. I got additional clarity about how I had treated my wife, as I saw her working tirelessly to find every way possible to remedy this. She made over 30 calls to the marketplace facilitator that weekend, alone! I am so blessed, honored, and proud to have her as my wife!

I also gained additional clarity through this negative event. I tried to accept that resisting this situation would only make it worse. Through my martial arts training, I had learned to be like water. Go with things. Don't resist. I got myself to a place of utmost confidence without any fear. I was even excited. I knew the Universe was there helping me along. I just had to remain patient. I was taking multiple opportunities throughout the day to calm my mind and and listen to my truest inner-self. I knew good things were coming!!!

Day 6

On Wednesday, I realized that we were almost one week in but still was able to retain a strongly positive attitude. I kept reminding myself of how exciting it will be to see sales on our online sales charts. I kept

looking online every few minutes all day and night,
excited for numbers other than zero to appear again!

LESSON 16: DON'T FIGHT THAT WHICH YOU CANNOT CONTROL.

Ultimately, we can only control ourselves. We truly can't control any other person or situation, in any relationship, be it personal or business. In addition, often, we can't even control ourselves well because our years of habits and coping mechanisms sneak up when you least expect them.

This is when I saw that this entire event was just a simple speed bump. That's all! By fighting with that which is unwanted and uncontrollable, I would have actually given it power and fueled its ability to hurt me, at least in my own mind, if not in the real world. I had to protect my mind. I couldn't succumb to the temptation to pity and wallow. I had to be strong and I was. I knew we would get through this just fine.

LESSON 17: DEBT IS ANOTHER WAY FOR SOMEONE ELSE TO CONTROL YOU.

I gained clarity about wanting to eliminate all the debt in my life. All the previous debt I took on was well-justified and reasonable. However, all it did was cost me sleep at night, worrying about how to pay it back in a situation such as this. I never saw bankruptcy as an option. I had borrowed that money and one way or another I was going to pay it back!

But, I learned that being debt-free would have allowed me to breeze through this situation. Just five years ago before all this happened, I had no debt whatsoever and had built a nice cushion of money in the business bank account. I imagined the same scenario occurring back then and it would have been no issue at all. Even three to six months of zero income would have been fine! We would have used the time to organize our warehouse and hone our systems for the future successes.

I was so happy to have learned this lesson, albeit the hard way. I knew *for certain* that I wanted to become 100% debt-free in the future. I knew I would find a way to do it, even if it meant hard decisions.

Day 7

I had convinced myself that I was learning patience. This was the only positive I could see at this point. That night we had some serious wind outside and I woke to find numerous branches all over the yard and driveway.

I compared this situation to that of the wind. I was the trees and this was knocking some dead branches off of me.

I regrouped and tried to take care of myself more. I had forgotten to do this over the past year or two. It was helpful.

I was proud to have had saved *some* backup cash, which I was now using up quite quickly to cover payroll, rent, and debt service.

I was seeing an equally positive result from all this negative. I felt that great things were coming! I decided to work to repair some relationships which I had let slide, with positive results.

LESSON 18: LET GO OF THINGS YOU CAN'T CHANGE.

I was getting so excited to see sales again... and money coming in again. As the current conditions popped into my head all through the day and night, I just kept telling them "blah, blah, blah" and replaced them with positive. I knew this was the way. It didn't help complaining about that which I could do nothing about.

It was obvious that there was nothing I could do. I just had to wait. So I let go... over and over. And over and over and over! 100s of times a day, the terror popped into my head, but repeatedly I replaced it with strong expectation of great things to come, with an emotional confidence behind it which made me believe it was inevitable!

I had some of the most wonderful times with my family on day 7. We really bonded. I was here and focused on them, because there was little else I could do. I was in a great mood, feeling fully excited for the future. I hadn't even told anyone outside of the company what happened. I was still ordering lots of product and had a full staff processing and shipping it all out to the marketplace facilitator's fulfillment centers. I had no doubt whatsoever that we would be back on again in a matter of days. I truly let go and it was wonderful!!

Day 8

By one week later, I had gained some good perspective.

LESSON 19: ALWAYS, ALWAYS, ALWAYS BE APPRECIATIVE OF WHAT YOU HAVE.

I vowed to never, ever again be sad about seeing sales number that I wasn't pleased with. I would be happy to see any sales numbers, at this point. I gained some real perspective and was enjoying the appreciation I was feeling for all our amazing customers who had trusted us to provide them with quality products and service.

I was feeling so deeply humbled for having been given the opportunity to have served them for the last eleven years. I knew that when we were turned back on, I would appreciate *every single one of our amazing customers* in a way I never had before. Perhaps I had gotten to a point where I took them for granted and nearly forgot they existed. After all, the dollar was driving every decision. It meant so much for me to have this clarity about the actual *people* who spend their hard-earned cash on our products. It's an honor to serve them!

LESSON 20: DON'T UNDERESTIMATE YOUR HUMAN-NESS.

B y now, I started justifying things. I guess that's part of the bargaining stage of grief, and this certainly was an experience of grief unlike I had ever experienced before.

Day 9

I started seeing good things happening in other areas of my life and tried to justify that this was happening in order for me to see other areas of my life. Perhaps this was true, and, certainly, seeing the good in any/all areas of my life is good!

But I really didn't expect this to be a grief process. I see now that it was. In fact it was a really tricky one, because the hope that we would be turned on every minute kept hiding the grief, sort of camouflaging it. I was still checking, literally, 100 times a day to see if we were back on yet. But, as the days passed, the hope veil got thinner and dimmer and the grief got larger, stronger, and more intense.

I learned that I am human, and that this is a good thing, not to be underestimated. As much as I think I can work an unlimited number of hours, conceive the most brilliant new ideas, and be entirely unaffected by bumps in the road, none of that is actually true. It would just be another lie I had told myself, to get through things like this.

Why? Because it worked in the past - working more hours, conceiving new methods/systems, and ignoring the bad are what got me to my success. But by not realizing that I, too, have human-limitations, I became unaware of my own weaknesses, which were in fact opportunities for growth.

I believe, not unlike a tree, growing is our primary objective for life. As such, my own inability to see my human-ness clearly was a very real inhibitor to my own growth.

LESSON 21:
IF YOU CAN'T
MAKE YOURSELF
HAPPY, NOBODY
ELSE CAN.

I became disgusted with myself because I knew that the moment we were going to be turned back on I would be overwhelmingly happy, yet my ability to remain happy was declining day by day. I was sick to my stomach that I had given them this authority over my happiness! I wanted to take it back. I didn't know how. I questioned my strength to do so, but recognized that through learning all these lessons I was effectively doing so, even though it didn't feel like it. I knew I needed to find ways to make myself happy.

So, I looked for any possible way to bring joy to my life, see joy in the world, and be joy to the world. It worked! At first, this was challenging and my successes were minimal. But, with continued effort, I succeeded more and more. Then a sort of momentum came which kept me moving forward more than backward, in the joy department.

This was an essential element of surviving this bump. I easily justified that there was, in all actuality, *nothing* I could do about this, so why not choose to enjoy these moments of my life, instead of fill them with sadness, hatred, and negativity.

LESSON 22:
CARING FOR YOUR MOOD IS SOME OF THE MOST IMPORTANT WORK YOU CAN DO.

I learned that by maintaining a positive mental state-of-mind through this entire bump gave me the ability to remain calm, see things I otherwise couldn't have, introspect enough to write this book, and look back on this event without any regrets.

Had I lost my temper, made rash decisions, taken extremely reactive actions, or damaged relationships beyond repair, I wouldn't be able to be here writing this book now. I would be immersed with guilt and depression, which is never a place I want to be in my life! I live a guilt-free life and I continue to maintain it. Caring for my emotional mind was essential!

LESSON 23:
TAKE EXTREME ACTION WHEN EXTREME ACTION IS NECESSARY.

A s I was just writing this, I made a chart for myself indicating which day number corresponded with each date, since my raw notes were all date-based. It was really surprising to see for just how many days we were turned off! It was a VERY long time! I didn't realize when I was in it just how long it had been. I kept staying in my moment, in each hour, in each day.

Looking back, I would have taken much more extreme action much sooner had I known how long we were actually shut down.

I was thinking, just now too, that this was similar to someone getting laid off or furloughed from their job. But it really isn't - I still had to pay all the business bills, which were getting more and more dire by the day, *and* my own living expenses! With no knowledge of if/when we would ever be turned back on, it seemed impossible to take action.

But taking action was truly all I really could actually do. In fact, other than relaxing my running thoughts to keep my mindset clear and analyzing the situation (which I had done millions of times by now) taking action is the only thing we can actually *do* in this physical world we live in.

But, I'm also glad I didn't take inappropriately extreme action. There was one time, when the thought crossed my mind to get a flight out to either the office of the owner of the fulfillment business or the office of the owner of the improper intellectual property claimant to tell them the truth of this situation and beg my case. I'm so glad I didn't - I probably would have been accused of harassment and made a bad situation much, much worse!

LESSON 24: YOU CAN ALWAYS HOLD OFF AND DO SOMETHING LATER, BUT YOU CAN'T UN-DO SOMETHING.

This is actually a lesson I had learned decades ago, but brought back to light again during this bump. As a father and martial arts instructor, I have taught this lesson numerous times, especially regarding holding your tongue. It's always better to stop and thoroughly consider something you may want to be saying, especially if you're in a state of anger or sadness at the time. You can always choose to say it later (even five minutes later, if you want), but you can't ever, ever un-say or un-do something you have done.

So, in this case, I am very glad that I didn't take any

erratic or emotionally reactive actions during this time. However, I did learn to, perhaps, not wait as long as I did, before I took action. This comes back to Lesson 2 about balance - it is all about balance. When you lose your balance, you lose your ability to remain/become effective, in any situation.

LESSON 25: NEVER, EVER, EVER, EVER, EVER, EVER, EVER, EVER GIVE UP!

I wish I could say I had delayed action deliberately. But it was more than that - I actually felt paralyzed. I felt unable to act, because it seemed there was nothing I could do! I was blinded by the monstrosity of a black cloud that was blocking all remnants of sunlight! I felt I had done all I could and that my future was in someone else's hands.

While I hadn't given up, I did feel that I had done all I could and that any additional action at this time would be prohibitive without knowledge of how this was going to play out. I see now, going back and writing this, that only later on, when I really, really dug deep down into myself, could I see my own essence of what it means to be me, alive, human, and continuing this life regardless of what comes my way.

Day 10

I had additional insights, today, regarding Lesson 15 (*"**Through contrast we gain clarity and learn about ourselves.**"*). I certainly was learning that I didn't *ever* want to be in this type of situation again. I had started this business in 1997 to get myself out from under a series of tyrannical bosses at my previous jobs. I remember back then vowing to myself that I would never again have a boss other than myself and that I would always treat my employees the way I wish I had been treated, but wasn't.

LESSON 26: TAKE TIME TO SEE THE BIG PICTURE AND ADJUST TO ENSURE YOU'RE STILL ON-COURSE.

I could see clearly that I had failed at my vow! Through the decisions I made regarding debt and business directions, I had effectively placed myself back into the employ of another horrible boss! In fact, this was worse! I couldn't even quit! I was stuck! Trapped in a situation, where numerous people were counting on me to survive!

I learned that, as I come through this, I will continually take action to ensure I am *never again* in such a caged, helpless, and demoralizing situation. I needed to take small steps in the coming months and year, to move myself away from debt-held positions and single-income sources.

For the past five years, I had gotten caught up in

getting through the next crisis that I forgot to step back and ensure I was still moving in the right direction! This is ironic, because I had the same situation back in the mid-2000s, when I actually hired an awesome business coach who taught me this. But I failed to heed this lesson and I was now bitten by it again.

I'm so incredibly excited to re-read this entire book every single year, to help myself remember exactly how, what, and why I am living my life.

LESSON 27: KEEP A STRONG HOLD ON YOUR MIND.

O n Day 10, my mind was also struggling with the bargaining phase of grief. It was trying to draw conclusions from all sorts of events which had occurred just prior to being shut down. It was looking for patterns, trying to connect dots, and investigating every little detail.

I concluded that I had been entertaining some incredibly negative, ungrateful, and reactional thinking and behaviors just prior to Day 1. I remembered being short with people, raising my voice, not wholeheartedly helping someone who came to me for assistance (when I could have helped more), and even feeling frustrated by the normal crying of my two under-two-years-old children.

I had let my mind slip. I am typically very strong-minded, but somehow I succumbed to the temptation to slip. I even had let fear in: Fear that some of my software, which was running all the critical elements of this business, was broken and unable for me to repair. Fear that the babies crying would interrupt my programming in a way that I would make unknown mistakes causing bigger problems. Fear of letting my wife down. Fear of letting all my children down. Fear of being the problem with everything.

LESSON 28: THAT WHICH YOU LOVE WILL GROW WELL.

I learned through this introspection that in order to succeed again, I needed to love every element of this business just like the other areas of my life which were good.

I got really honest with myself and noticed that I had not been giving this business the love it deserved, certainly not the love I had been giving it in the past. I had been viewing it as a burden, an anchor which was keeping me from doing things I wanted to do in my life. I was even resentful about having bought out my partner's half.

But I learned that this approach not only didn't feel good, but it wasn't working! It was literally the opposite of what the business needed from me. And what *I* needed from me. I consciously thought about every element of my business: The old internet side, the new ecommerce side, so many trusting customers, the loyal and productive employees, the generous lenders, the quality manufacturers and vendors, and the awesome marketplace and fulfillment systems I had been enjoying.

It felt so good to see them all in this light. To *truly* value every one of these elements, as I knew I really did deep down, but I had just forgotten. It was time to let the bitterness roll off and replace it with love - an honest, deep love for every element of this business.

For many, many hours, on day 10, I just let this love grow and grow, and it did, as if on its own. I am certain I always had that love inside and was actually now just allowing it to flow. Apparently, I had resisted its flow in the past, which created all sorts of issues in me, other people, and the business itself. Most of all, I still recall just how awesome it felt to feel love for all these elements of this business!

I remember imagining individual customers carefully choosing to spend their hard-earned money with us and being delighted by the products we had provided in such a quality way. I thanked them in my mind for giving us the opportunity to delight them, for trusting us to serve their needs. I sent them well-wishes and happiness!

I saw so many of our wonderful employees, both present and past, who really did such a good job for the company in so many ways. I sent them all love in my mind, wishing them all the best in their lives today and always!

I felt so humbled that so many lenders would trust me enough to pay them back, that they would loan me money. I felt honored to be able to pay them back and to use their money to help me grow this business. I saw myself paying each one back with such a happy smile on my face and joy that they had allowed me to use their money!

I imagined all my vendors and manufacturers taking their own risks to design and create such wonderful products for me to source from them. I prayed in thankfulness for their willingness to work with us and allow us to represent their product well. I am deeply blessed to have such a wonderful network of providers!

I considered even this marketplace facilitator and fulfillment provider who shut us down. I realized that this is their business and for whatever reason they did, they took these steps to ensure their best desired outcomes. I felt so appreciative that they would even have let me work with them for these past eleven years and that they allowed me to submit an appeal for this case. I understood that they were only doing what they thought was right and I happened to be a small little cog in their system. I felt so grateful to have their partnership!

Day 11

I noticed that we had lost a very large Internet client during that same time and the only time they had available to talk with me about it was, literally, the exact moment we were being shut down on Day 1.

This coincidence seemed too real and I had written in my notes today that "In the past I would have thought the Universe was conspiring against me, but now I see it was just my own vibrations at that moment! I'm getting happy again and things are flowing so well!"

Then, within minutes of writing this, I got notified that I had been approved for a short-term loan to help get through this. I know... another loan. But borrowing more money was truly my only option!

I also was reminiscing of events ten, 15, even 20 years ago, realizing how much of those times were good. I see now that I really did have a good life then in so many ways. Maybe I had convinced myself otherwise, but nothing can take away the good that was.

Day 12

My mind started dreaming of all the good that could come: Having the debt gone, getting a condo in Florida, maybe even continuing the pilot training I had started seven years ago but abandoned when money got tight.

LESSON 29: HALF-FULL IS BETTER THAN HALF-EMPTY.

I concluded that my past thinking about fear of not having enough money had programmed my subconscious mind to cause me to act in ways that would keep me from having enough money. This included taking more loans, dropping sales, and this current shutdown!

I remembered when I started this ecommerce business, how every single sale was delightful! Lately, however, it never seemed to be enough! This negative view had been causing me to pull away from opportunities and insights which I otherwise would have seen and capitalized on, perhaps even including the ability to have predicted and remedied this type of intellectual property claim before it could have even happened!

I realized I somehow had fallen for the half-empty mindset! How disgusting! Somehow it snuck into my head when I wasn't looking! I was *always* the optimist

- ALWAYS! I don't know when or how it happened but it did, and it was time to call the exterminator!

I heard in a motivational recording on YouTube that, "Beauty, quiet, and nature allow you to enjoy your good fortune." So, I took some time away in nature and felt even more refreshed and ready-to-go!

Day 13

I woke up several times through the night with nightmares of people who were wishing for my failure. They were spreading lies about me being a horrible person, which hurt so much because I have *always* been a kind, helpful, loving, and caring person in every aspect of my entire life!

LESSON 30: ONLY SUCCESS CAN HELP OTHERS. FAILURE CAN'T HELP ANYONE.

I realized that these dreams were, in effect, me failing so that these people could see me fail, in order that they could see that I was a good person, not the evil person they claimed I was when I succeeded. I decided then to not allow any sort of failure for anyone else. My failure doesn't help anyone. Only my success can help others, even those who wish me ill will.

Being a loving and caring person, somehow I suspect that my mind concluded that my own success was somehow hurting, not helping, other people. I think I had fallen for the non-popular one-size-pie model, where all my success is actually taking from someone else's ability to succeed. I know this to be a lie -- History has shown the pie just keeps growing, over, and over, and over, and my bigger and bigger piece doesn't take from anyone else but instead

causes the pie to grow, so there is more for everyone!
Maybe somehow I forgot this.

LESSON 31: EVERYTHING IS ALWAYS WORKING OUT PERFECTLY.

This was a hard lesson to understand, because it seemed so contrary to the reality I was living. But I had spent some time on day 13 thinking about every seemingly-impossible event in my past, and concluding, accurately, that I had always gotten through it. And, in the vast majority of these cases, things actually worked out better due to the conflict.

I recalled having read "How to Stop Worrying and Start Living" by Dale Carnegie, perhaps 25 years ago, where he studied 1000s of things that people worried about going "wrong." When analyzing the actual data, it was something like 96% never happened and three percent happened, but actually produced better results. And the one percent that did happen negatively weren't nearly as damaging as anticipated.

I concluded in my mind that there was *no way* this wasn't "right!" It really was the perfect challenge for me. Things always worked out for me in the past, and this would be no exception! So, so, so many times, this was true! In fact there was never an exception, where a serious situation I had worried about in the past didn't come to pass in a good way! I decided it would be so fun to see how this would all work out!

I told my Mom and Dad today about the situation. They both were incredibly loving and caring all through this entire situation! Dad continued to stay in close contact, reassuring me at every point, helping me keep my mind positive. Mom immediately gave us grocery money, then later heating oil money, and continued grocery money, since we were quickly using up every penny of savings we had by just paying the mortgage every month. They both gave a monumental piece of themselves to me, which was very meaningful. I couldn't have gotten through this without my parents. I'm so incredibly blessed to have their love in my life and I thank them with all that I am!!!

Day 14

Fourteen days is two weeks! TWO WEEKS! At this point, I clearly recall thinking that this just simply *can't* go on much longer. I felt it was impossible! At the time, little did I know it would go on *so* much longer! Oh my!

As I write this, I am trying to find every way possible to convey to you the extremely serious nature of this situation. If I had no debt and extra money in the bank, it would definitely have *NOT* been a big deal! That's where I was five years ago. But now, with every personal credit card I had literally at the maximum charge, every line of credit I could find "max'ed" out also, every business card at it limit, every dollar of every vendor's credit lines maxed, two crazy-loans (where you sign your life away and if you miss a single *daily* payment, they take it all), and this significant balance remaining short-term (meaning the *weekly* repayment amount was over 50% of what we had been selling each week!) loan, which just so happened to be from the same company who was my market-place facilitator *and* my fulfillment provider!

Servicing these debts, meaning paying the min-imums, was a lot of money every month! And the business was only selling approximately 50% of what we had sold last year. So, that left about half to pay the marketplace facilitator their commission, the fulfillment provider their order fees, employees, rent, insurance, utilities, taxes, and all other miscellan-eous expenses. You can do the math. That left noth-ing. Not that I was worried about that - I have lived on nothing before and am glad doing it. And, luckily the Martial Arts School, which I took over ten years ago from my Grandmaster when he retired, was doing ok enough that it paid about half my monthly living expenses! But, we got *really* good at living on day-old bread ($0.88 a bag fed us all for one to two days), heat-ing only one room in the house, buying *nothing* outside of the immediate necessities, and making rolling around the living room floor with the kids our daily recreation activity!

LESSON 32: THERE'S NO SUCH THING AS A SURE-THING.

No, the real issue was that every dollar of sales used up that much inventory, after expenses, it didn't allow for re-buying anything! However, I still had some inventory left, which I was planning on selling down to about half during this holiday season, and using the proceeds from it to entirely pay off the marketplace fulfillment provider and the two crazy loans. This would have dropped my monthly cash flow to service the remaining debt enough to have left more than enough to buy more profitable products and dig myself out of this hole! I was so excited to do this. And, there were still three more weeks before Cyber-Monday, the start of the holiday season. So, I had ample time before really having to be concerned.

I was certain that I would be able to pull it off. I am always an optimist, except when I'm not! I was so sure I could do this. There had been five-plus years of hard work (twenty, really, leading to this point) and it was *finally* my time to get out from under the debt burden and this was going to be my holiday season. I had put all my eggs into that basket. I spoke so confidently. I just *knew* I could do it.

But I'm afraid that my doing it was really a rebellion from all that I *didn't want*, rather than a focused desire on what I *did want.* I learned there's a big difference! Focusing on getting away-from or out-of what you don't want is really quite the same, to your subconscious mind, as continuing that which you don't want.

Instead I should have focused on what I really wanted. How it would have felt. How wonderful it would be. But I didn't even know I wasn't thinking this way. I just wanted to be out from the burden I had carried so long, that which kept me awake night after night, that which weighted down my heart and made me dull.

Had I been a bit less optimistic, I would have seen that there really is no such thing as a sure-thing. This holiday season was to be no exception. I should have accepted this reality and had a back-up plan. I should have done things to more ensure this 'sure thing' rather than just hope it was a sure thing. Again, I didn't know at the time. But now, I have certainly learned this lesson. I am responsible for ensuring my own 'sure things' in life - there's no magic. It starts with my mind then continues through my actions.

LESSON 33:
SUFFERING DOES
NOT ENTITLE
YOU TO SUCCESS.
SUCCESS
ENTITLES YOU
TO SUCCESS.

Somehow, I think I was feeling that I deserved this holiday season after all the hell I had been through. I thought I had paid my price. I thought that somehow my suffering entitled me to success. I felt like it was finally my time.

Little did I know that I had built up so much negative momentum all these years, that, while it was slowing and starting to turn around, it was still quite negative! I had much, much more work to do to turn it around. I needed to apply my entire mental and physical focus to ensuring my success, not just thinking that my past suffering somehow would bring me to success.

Once again, I didn't know this at the time. (I know, I keep saying this, but it's true!) I suspect *many* people remain perplexed about their seeming "worst luck in the world" where things just seem to keep going wrong for them day after day, year after year, and decade after decade. It's because they were like me -- they built negative momentum and slowing it takes concerted, disciplined, focused, regular mental work, which leads to the proper, effective physical work.

LESSON 34:
ONLY MY FOCUS
WILL BRING
MY SUCCESS.
NOTHING
ELSE WILL.

Compared to where I was going a year or two ago, I was doing great before this bump. Because of that, I thought I had changed direction. I can see now that I hadn't. I only slowed the negative momentum, but I was still going in the wrong direction. I didn't know. I can see more clearly now. I see that I am still not in positive momentum yet, but that I am just about at zero, finally! I just keep pressing on, now, and know only my focus will bring my success. NOTHING ELSE!!

LESSON 35: TRUST YOUR TEAM, WITH YOUR HEART.

I decided to focus on trusting all the other players, who were involved in this with me: My wife, my employees, my customers, my marketplace facilitator/fulfillment provider, my lenders, and my vendors. I trusted that they would help get through this. After all, it was in their best interest too.

But that was a logical approach. I needed to trust them with my heart. I needed to know and feel their energy moving with mine toward an outcome that would be in the best interest of all of us. I kept hearing an old meditation I used to practice 20 years ago saying, "May the best for all involved occur." Rather than just hope this, I started trusting this.

I knew in my heart that there was an outcome which would do just that... bring to all those involved the best possible results. My mental mind stopped chattering, when I did this. At least it stopped chattering about all those people involved. I stopped faulting any of them. I stopped if-only-ing (you know, if only person A had done this or company B hadn't done that). I stopped wanting *them* to be different for *my* benefit.

I started trusting that each of them had their own hearts, their own dreams, their own desires, and their own outcomes. I began a sort of praying, that every single person involved in this situation, directly and indirectly, would be able to have the best possible outcome from it!

I don't know for certain if this worked, but I strongly suspect it did. However, I am *certain* that it definitely affected my outlook. It definitely changed my heart, in a way. It gave me contrast and clarity, and took my mind off myself - that is, my currently lacking situation. Instead it put my mind on a much bigger, greater picture of success which was right around the corner for all of us!

LESSON 36: FOLLOW THE PATH OF LEAST RESISTANCE.

I had heard it said that the path of least resistance is also the path of greatest success. This initially confused me, because I equated least resistance to being lazy. But that's not it at all! Least resistance means driving the best route to work, taking the road with the less traffic, and following the most direct route. There is nothing lazy about this -- it simply makes sense. So, I started applying it to my life, mentally.

I realized today that, in my mind, *I* was very much the resistance that this business didn't need most! I, myself, was, in my thinking, seeing this business as an anchor, something I had to drag around, a mess I had to clean up, full of headaches from my past. I couldn't even go into the office without getting physically nauseous.

None of this was the business' fault! The business was good, strong, and wonderful! I had just simply allowed negativity to enter my mind about it from past events and experiences with many other people. I felt hurt, betrayed, abused, and terribly disrespected. Somehow, I let these past assaults tamper with my love for this business!

By doing this, *I* was the resistance to the business' success! I was its greatest enemy! Of course, I didn't know this, and likely would have told anyone they were crazy if they had tried to tell me this. Only through this situation was I able to see clarity around this. Only through sinking deeper and deeper in this crazy bump, was I able to identify my own culpability in the direction and resulting outcome of this business!

This was so liberating for me to realize today! I realized that this business *truly was* the path of least resistance, itself. If I would just get out of the way, and allow it to flow, it would! If I could continue to remember that this business is *not* the problem, but the *solution*, I would be just fine!

Day 15

Since currently I'm writing this after-the-fact, I'm going to take a moment to jump out of the timeline to help prepare you for what's coming. Over the next days and weeks, you'll notice lots of "ups" and "downs" (both minor and major) in my outlook, mood, confidence, and even self-esteem. This is because I had absolutely no idea, at any point in this entire episode, as to when, or even if, we would ever be turned back on again.

Without any sort of concrete "light at the end of the tunnel," my ability to remain steadfast was severely challenged. What comes ahead is an account of both the challenges and my attempts to remain balanced, whole, and intact, while learning lessons through the process. I hope that by sharing this with you now, you will indulge my tribulations in the coming pages and tolerate what may seem like an unending roller-coaster, as that is *exactly* what it felt like! The end does come, I assure you!

I'm feeling so grateful and thankful today! I'm feeling like, in dozens of way, I have been given another chance at life! I feel like I was heading in the wrong direction so many times, and somehow I always turned myself around and things always looked up!

Day 16

I feel like I have been through a war with myself today. I had such old ways of thinking about money. I had learned to see money as a simple cause-and-effect. If I did x, then y would happen. Of course this is true, but there's much more to it than this. I learned today that I must be predisposed to the success. I must be ready to accept it, ready to *allow* it to come in, and ready to cast off my old resisting ways.

LESSON 37:
THERE'S ALWAYS
A MUCH BIGGER
PICTURE. SEEING
IT OFTEN HELPS.

I remember back when I was much younger. Money never, ever bothered me. Never did I have money concerns. Sure, I had money issues, but I forgot about them as fast as I thought of them, and things always did work out perfectly somehow -- every time!

Somehow, I had gotten my mind stuck down in the muck of money and life, and hurt and sadness, and finger-pointing and name-calling. None of this has anything to do with anything!

I realized, today, that there is truly *NOTHING I CAN DO* about the timing of this situation. I can't make them turn me on. I couldn't have made them turn me off. It was entirely out of my hands. I can, now, only make the best of it!

In fact, as I thought bigger and bigger, I realized that *if this had to happen*, there truly couldn't have been a better time! Just after I got out from two large financial issues that had burdened the company for the past four years, and just before the awesome holiday boom season!

I reminded myself how much I'm growing and learning from all this! I see my mind getting stronger and stronger! My ability to remain calm and in-balance (harmony/alignment with myself) during these undesirable conditions, is really amazing me!

I see that my little life and its problems are so, so, so teeny compared to all the amazing wonderfulness and goodness in this whole world! I just let that sink in! And it did!

I'm feeling so much appreciation for my martial arts training and all the balance it brings me! The people, the community, the techniques, and my Grandmaster - they all bring me balance.

Day 18

Just heard from one of my largest vendors that this happened to them too, right now! It confirms that this is part of a much larger issue/problem occurring outside what I or we could affect. Maybe, since the complaints originated from China, this is in some sort of response to the recent trade tariffs that were applied. Or maybe someone, so high up in the world government working, got mad at someone else, and somehow this trickled down to us? In any case, we weren't going through this alone.

We had beautiful discussions and bonded in ways that were so meaningful. I hoped I could give them some of the things I had been learning. They supported me so graciously. I felt so incredibly blessed to have their friendship!!!

Day 19

I was still thinking bigger and bigger and realized just how good of a life I have had! I felt so amazed at how much opportunity to proactively control my emotions I am getting through this bump!

I saw that I'm learning that the negative emotions I feel now are simply an indication that I was out of harmony with myself. As I realized this and re-entered harmony with myself, things felt better, and they actually were!

I even went so far with the big picture that I nearly convinced myself that none of this is even real! I saw clearly that these dollars are simply numbers on computer screens. Numbers which are *like* money, but aren't actually dollars! Hmm... That is a bit hard to write, right now, because it seems too "far out" but I do still remember having that thought and feeling, so real that it actually *was* real to me!

LESSON 38: DON'T MAKE ANY FAST STARTS OR STOPS, WHEN DRIVING IN SLIPPERY WEATHER.

I learned that this situation is like being in an incredibly disastrous winter storm! Of course, I should have seen it coming and stayed home (no debt and money in the bank), but I didn't! I was out driving in the storm -- Driving to save my life and the lives of those I love.

So, I had to take it easy... go with it... literally, *GO WITH IT!* Realize that I can't really do much other than keep a slow, steady momentum. If I were to hit the brakes hard or gas pedal quickly, I would spin out and cause permanent damage. I had to just go with it and not allow anything to take my eyes off the road. I couldn't let anything affect my emotions. I just had to know that I would get through the storm and be ok.

LESSON 39: NEVER, EVER GET ON ANYONE'S CASE WHEN THEY'RE DOING THEIR BEST.

Day 20

I made a promise to myself to never, ever get on anyone's case when they are doing their best! I saw that I had done this far too many times. Somehow, I felt it was my responsibility to "educate" them as to the better way of doing things. I felt that I had everything to lose and therefore they needed to do exactly as I specified. I felt that I could forgive their mistakes only so far.

I learned today that when I got on other people's cases, even in a well-meaning spirit, that I somehow broke my own harmony with myself. Somehow, I got myself off-balance and recovering took hours or days. This became incredibly counter-productive! *Maybe* (but unlikely) I helped them learn something to do better, but I got in my own way so much in doing so. I would spend hours re-hashing the whole conversations in my mind. Eventually, I always concluded that I had not been kind enough, or caring enough, or gentle enough in my approach.

So, today, I learned to stop that. Just stop it altogether! Of course, help people learn, but never, ever, ever get on someone's case when they are trying hard. Instead, I now blame myself, in a good way. I see that both I and they *are* good, kind, loving, caring people and, together, we will grow and improve and succeed. By treating them in an adversarial manner, I actually caused strife. I created disharmony and resistance in the flow.

This is a big lesson! I think I somehow knew it in my heart, all these years, but it took this bump for me to stop justifying my behavior as effective, responsible, or necessary. Instead, I now see that a loving approach will always produce loving fruit for all involved.

Day 21

I realized that I had been listening to many motivational speakers online lately and one of their themes was to meditate. I hadn't meditated in years. So, I decided to start meditating again... Today!

So, I dug out an old meditation tape I used to love

and gave it a try. Initially, my first benefit was nearly complete removal of pain from my body. This was pain caused by the stress of this situation, which I had been harboring inside myself.

I see, now, in writing this book, that if the only benefit I received was meditating again regularly, then the whole bump was worth it!

The second benefit I received was amazing dreams all night of the marketplace facilitator fixing their error and turning us back on. I literally saw a person doing it, in my dream, and it felt so wonderful!!!

The third benefit was a dream of some sort of a book I had written! In fact, it was the initial seed for writing this book!

I meditated a second time today, and found things were working out everywhere in my life, like magic! I was so calm and receptive and loving in all my interactions. This made the day just wonderful!

LESSON 40:
YOU HAVE
EVERYTHING
YOU NEED INSIDE
YOURSELF.

Day 22

I saw clearly that I had all I needed inside of me. I never, really needed anyone else's advice. I asked for it because I thought it was important, or the right thing to do, or that they knew more than I did.

But the truth is that I truly had access to all the information I needed in the form of impulses and inclinations, when I was balanced and in harmony with myself.

I realized that I *truly AM* an incredibly good, kind, caring, loving, and helpful person. I knew this at one level, but at another, I just couldn't believe it. I had been so beat down by life over these past five to ten years that I questioned myself, even. I seemed to forget who I was and how to even reconnect with myself.

I had a dream tonight of someone physically hurting me and actually fighting back! I hadn't ever had this type of dream -- I was always the victim. It felt so good to be defending myself, standing up for my own merit and value and worth. It was about time!

LESSON 41: TRUTH INCLUDES BOTH OPPORTUNITIES AND THREATS, NOT JUST ONE OR THE OTHER.

I woke up remembering a past employee, years ago, who very kindly had warned me about the potential of this exact type of situation occurring. She cautioned me in many ways, but I didn't listen. I only saw the positive potential and couldn't understand the negative risks. I wish now, that I had listened to her more.

Of course, all things have opposites: up/down, left/right, summer/winter, dark/light, yin/yang. How silly of me to look at only the opportunities without including the threats!

Somehow, I felt that by acknowledging risks I was somehow allowing them to exist. But this isn't true at all. Accepting the reality of risks, addressing them so they are minimized, and moving forward optimistically is really the formula for success in any and all areas of life.

Day 23

I decided to take a couple days away, to clear my mind and reset my mood, energy, and balance. So, I checked my hotel app on my phone and found a place about an hour away which was running a special sale. $50 a night seemed like a good deal and something I could justify. This was a big thing for me to do, because I always feel like I'm taking food out of the mouth of my family. But I concluded that taking care of myself and giving myself balance would be the best course of action at this time.

LESSON 42:
YOU GET WHAT
YOU PAY FOR!

E ven though it was really cold out, I went to the beach and had a great walk. Then I went to my hotel room. It was really, really not nice! I felt so uncomfortable - there was a car jacked up without any wheels on it, suspicious people all around, and many signs that said they weren't responsible for anything being stolen, including your car itself. The room smelled horrible and had a strange one-foot wide balcony outside the sliding door, which connected all the rooms via the outside. It just didn't feel right, so I went and talked to the manager and he agreed to give me a refund.

I drove around a bit and found another one up the street, which was the complete opposite in every way. The attendant gave me a fair price for it, too ($109). I then took myself to a nice Korean dinner then to a small local concert. I so enjoyed the dedication the artists had to their work! I went back and enjoyed sleeping in the nice room.

At dinner, my fortune cookie said: "Greed leads to poverty!" At the time, it seemed like a nice quote, but

I didn't see any connection to me. I never saw myself as greedy. In fact, I was still feeling guilt from taking this time away for myself.

However, now that I'm writing this, I can see that trying to get the cheapest room possible was in itself a form of greed. It was trying to get more than a good value for all involved. I was taught this lesson well -- you get what you pay for!

Day 24

So, I woke up the next morning invigorated and ready for the day. I planned on just seeing what felt right to do. I took a nice shower and was going to catch up on some work and maybe watch a movie, then go out to another concert that night.

Then, I got an email from the marketplace facilitator! I was so excited. However, it was a notice that my account had been deactivated again (it never even got turned on the first time) because I had such a large variance in recent sales compared to my norm! I couldn't believe this! But, I felt hopeful that addressing this might prompt someone there to review the first case and just turn us back on!

So, I wrote a thoughtful reply regarding this issue and also addressing the previous issue again. I included a bunch of additional documentation they had requested in their generic email to me, hoping this would help, too!

I got some work done, watched a movie on the hotel TV, but then I got lonely and did what I've done *so* many times before -- I skipped the concert that night and came home early! I so miss my family when I'm away, but when I'm engrossed in the day-to-day, I just need some time away. Guess I never need as much time away as I think. Or maybe, I'm just good at recovering quickly.

Either way, I felt so excited to have had some contact from them. It felt like it would be just another couple days at most before this bump would be a distant memory!

Since I left the hotel early, I thought I would check with them if there was a way they could not charge me for the second night. I realized I was there all day and they couldn't have rented the room to anyone else. But something inside me thought I might as well ask. After all, I was encumbered by this horrible situation which was starting to get a bit scary!

LESSON 43: ABUNDANT PEOPLE AREN'T BEGGARS.

The clerk said a polite "no," but suggested I call the next morning to talk to the manager, who might be willing to make an exception for me. The whole ride back home, I thought about this. It was like there was some sort of internal war going on inside my soul. Maybe it was my soul vs. my mind? Or my logic vs. my emotion? Or my new-self vs. my old-self? I don't know, but it was very real.

Part of me was feeling that I needed pity - that I deserved it almost! I got such clarity about how this had become part of my thinking as a child, being horribly treated by my classmates. I think I had learned ways of getting pity to survive and avoid painful attention. I felt like this bump was a sort of survival and the pity I needed would somehow help my young-self feel appreciated or at least not abused.

But as I continued to think about this, I realized that holding a beggar-mindset was actually lack-based thinking, focused on failure, weakness, and not having enough. I had worked so hard over my lifetime, and especially the past five years, to believe that I am enough and that I live an incredibly abundant life in every way! I wasn't about to let this get in the way of my momentum!

But as I continued to think about this, I realized that holding a beggar-mindset was actually lack-based thinking, focused on failure, weakness, and not having enough. I had worked so hard over my lifetime, and especially the past five years, to believe that I *am* enough and that I live an incredibly abundant life in every way! I wasn't about to let this get in the way of my momentum!

So, I concluded that there was no way I was going to call and talk to the manager! They did what they promised to do, and did it very well! It was entirely my choice to leave early. It would actually be morally wrong to ask them for anything more. We had a beautiful balance in the transaction... win-win, as it is so popularly called. If I were I to have put my finger on the scale in this manner, I would have seriously disturbed the beautiful balance that existed!

LESSON 44: FOCUS ON NOT-ENOUGH MAKES GREED. FOCUS ON MORE-THAN-ENOUGH ALLOWS THE FLOW.

I don't need pity. I don't need to beg. I have more than enough! I am not in a position of lack! My old childhood training taught me to try to get all I could from everyone. But I have more than enough and felt so strongly that it was wasn't right to ask the hotel for more. In fact, I concluded that it would have been a type of stealing, which was absolutely not something I would ever do!

As I dug deeper into myself, I realized that making money was actually a sort of compensation for my low self-esteem which was really a disconnect with my true-self and came from my mistreatment as a child. Again, I was amazed how things that happened decades ago were still shaping my thinking and behavior! I was so delighted to have worked through this thinking and learned this lesson!

Making lots of money was a sort of way of getting back at the people who put me down so often as a child. But I have no need to do that now. I am ok and good. I have no need to be greedy. Being greedy would just cut off my abundant flow because my mind would be acting from a position of lack. Not having enough makes me greedy. But I have more than enough. There is, therefore, no need to focus on having. Instead, I focus on allowing myself to grow and be more every day, and, in doing so, more comes in every day. The difference here may seem slight, but it is truly critical.

Focus on not-enough makes greed. Focus on more-than-enough allows the flow. I have more than enough. I have abundance in all areas of my life!

LESSON 45: NEVER WORRY ABOUT MONEY AND THERE WILL BE NOTHING TO WORRY ABOUT REGARDING MONEY.

This lesson may seem obvious, but it truly wasn't to me. I was so deep in the last 25 days of zero sales, meaning lots of borrowed money, just to pay the bills, and was starting to worry about if I would "make it" through.

But this lesson came to me, almost as a sort of vision or message. It seems like one of those "a-ha" moments because it is so simple and succinct!

Think about it for a moment, please... If you never

worry about money, then you just won't have anything to worry about regarding money. I know, it almost seems circular or redundant, but what we think about is our choice. Worry is simply one thing we can think about. So, choosing to think of abundance, joy, prosperity, love, and growth will displace all fears and worries regarding lack of money. By doing this, consciously, I was learning that it felt really good to not be worrying about money. Abundance is everywhere!

In fact, by not worrying, I had nothing to worry about! All those fears which had been taunting me were simply gone. There was no room for them, because my mind was delighting itself with thoughts of plenty - so much plenty that I even have some to share! What a good feeling. What a wonderful way to focus my mind!

Day 25

I woke up this Monday morning with a clear thought in my mind:

LESSON 46: EVERYTHING WAS MY FAULT.

I t wasn't in a pity sort of way, or a "look at how bad everything is for me." It was more of a self, internal belief, which ended up liberating me.

I had somehow, in my sleep, concluded that this entire issue was entirely my fault. I had caused it. I had created it.

I cannot blame anyone but myself -- not my wife, my employees, my vendors, the marketplace facilitator, even the sneaky rights-owner who initiated the claim against us!

I accepted this responsibility today, on day 25! I prohibited myself from that back-mind thinking which says things like, "if only this..." or "no, that..." or "why didn't they..." or "he/she should have..." Enough was enough. This was my entire fault. It truly was! It is my business and I am the only person in the world who loves it like I do, and knows it like I do to be able to take care of it. I am here. It happened. It is my fault. Period!

As I allowed this to sink in, without any resistance

to it, I realized it was true. Looking back, I saw that I could have had much better oversight of the procedures we were following to avoid such situations. I saw that I had actually looked the other way regarding things like this, because I had convinced myself that I was too busy building the business. But this element of the business was just as critical (more so, now) as that I had been doing.

LESSON 47: YOU'VE GOT TO KEEP ALL THE PLATE SPINNING, WITHOUT LETTING ANY DROP.

I had a boss years ago, who taught me this lesson. I just had forgotten it. He said to imagine you were the plate-spinner in the circus, who had numerous plates spinning on wooden sticks. Just as one slows down, you have to give it just enough spin to keep it going, while keeping all the others going. You can't let any two get too slow, or you won't be able to spin them both at the same time, so you have to always be watching everything all the time and putting in little spins here and there constantly.

If I had been following this lesson, I would have never allowed an intellectual property claim to have popped up. I would have had methods for dealing with them quickly and promptly, if they did occur. I would have taken steps to ensure that we were regularly checking the online listings, so when these unscrupulous people "hijack" a legitimate listing to become "their own" by convincing the marketplace facilitator that the product brand legally belongs to them, we would have simply removed our stock and deleted the listing. I would have built even better systems to ensure no mistakes were made on our part when we did our initial research of the listings.

There was so much I could have done, but I let those plates fall. In fact, I looked the other way when they fell, so I wouldn't have to hear the sound of them breaking! But now I was stuck cleaning up the sharp, dangerous mess of broken glass pieces!

So, I decided to take even better care of myself. I did some really deep meditations again today, and it seemed like everything was just flowing so well again!!

It turns out that taking full, 100% responsibility for all this truly freed me! I had been caught in a seductive trap of avoidance and didn't even know it! Now, I was free -- because the only person I can ever truly control is myself and now I had taken back all the power because if this was to be resolved, it would have to be done by *me!*

Day 27

Today was a day of letting things sink in.

The marketplace facilitator got back to us and said we hadn't addressed their concerns adequately in *both* of the account suspensions (the initial rights-owner claim and the new sales variance alert). So, I dug down, and put together some really powerful internal systems to help me ensure this would never happen again. I communicated them confidently to both cases, as they were looking for proof that we would never again allow this to happen, and felt so certain we would be back on in a matter of hours!! After all, Cyber Monday was just ten days away and my team was working so hard sending out so much additional product to be ready for it! There was no doubt in my mind.

I had a realization that I would be just as happy with my family, if we were to lose all we have and went back to a very simple lifestyle. We might even be happier! So why not be this happy now? So I decided I was... and I was! Yay!!

I saw that many life events over the past five years had made me feel like a victim. I got myself stuck in this mindset and ended up becoming a victim, in every possible way! I am so glad to be aware of this and over it! I am my own successful life-creator again!!

I am strong and capable and confident. I am a black belt under my Grandmaster's training, which was no small feat! I have and will always get through everything! Everything that looks bad, I turn to good. I always have and always will. Everything truly always works out for me!!! Yay!!

I understood that my wife is my secret weapon! She has never, ever, not even once worried about money. Even now through all this. She is steadfast and strong in her confidence in me and our upcoming success in every area of our lives! She is just amazing!!!

I was seeing so clearly how all this was a good thing! It led me to realize the power of my mind! I deliberately focused my mind on incredible success for several minutes and it felt amazing. That happy, positive flow lasted over 30 minutes later! It was some of the most amazing momentum I have ever felt!

I could understand, at a deep soul-level, that our account being turned back on *truly was* the path of least resistance. I could see how all this learning would be so much more of a better opportunity than the small price of one month of lost sales! Yay!!

I remembered how I had lost everything once in my past, a few years back. I can lose it again even and be just fine! This type of thinking released resistance and focused me on where I am, and allowed me to flow again!

What a good day!

Day 28

I had another amazing day of positive energy! I am not a victim in any way! I am a champion!!!

LESSON 48: A SUCCESSFUL TEAM MUST VIBRATE IN HARMONY.

I saw that I was not in harmony with my wife before this, because I hadn't been trusting her to complete her work at the levels I was expecting. But instead of coaching her, talking with her, building systems to help her, or even taking some of the load off so she could find her own balance, I didn't open myself up to her. I was fearful from past relationships.

Now, I am building her up. I am loving her! I am trusting her! And it is all going so well!!

LESSON 49:
EVEN POSITIVE THINKING ABOUT A NEGATIVE SITUATION IS STILL A NEGATIVE RESPONSE.

I realized that a large element of this team was the marketplace facilitator themselves. I was not in harmony with them. I was thinking about them all the time because the negativity of the situation was incredibly real!!! I saw that my attempts to think positively about all this were simply in response to the negativity that existed, and therefore were actually a focus on the negative by responding to it.

If none of this had happened, I wouldn't be trying to think so positively to overcome the negative. I would just be going on with my day, as normal! And I certainly wouldn't be talking about it all the time, neither positively nor negatively.

So, I decided to do just that. I made a rule for my-self that I would not discuss this situation at all with anyone... not even my wife, and especially not even myself! I simply would not discuss it... absolutely nothing about it. Instead, I would replace that time with happy, enjoyable, fun thoughts and actions!

LESSON 50: SOMEHOW THIS IS PERFECT. EVERYTHING LED ME TO WHERE I AM NOW, SO JUST ENJOY AND LOVE IT.

I realized that somehow this crazy bump was exactly right. It was exactly what I needed. I could see that everything that happened had led me to a very single moment... NOW. There was no going back and the majority of the future would depend on my thinking, so I decided to enjoy NOW and love NOW!

Day 29

I continued my lesson 50 thinking with ideas like: Why not me? Why not now? I am successful. I always have been my whole life. This is no different! Nobody else is better than I am. I can do anything!!!!

I saw how I had let and allowed my mental focus to get all confused, dizzy, blurry, and scattered over past few years. It was time to get back my strong focus and momentum again, regardless of what happens in my life!!!!

LESSON 51: DO ALL YOU CAN EACH DAY... THEN REST.

There was nothing I could do about this anymore now. I had done all I could. So I chose to be happy and do things other than worry. I chose to be proud of my courage in how I have been handling it and enjoy!

There is something to be said for doing your best! Of course, do all you can. Give it your all. Work smart and hard! But, when you've done that, it's time to *STOP!* There is a point of diminishing returns, when you press yourself past your limit. This is very clear in physical work, but not so much so of mental work. But the lesson applies identically. When you've done all you can, stop, take a break, and rest! Allow yourself to come back in to balance! (There's that Lesson 2 again... Maybe I should have entitled the book "Balance" instead?!)

LESSON 52: DON'T THINK YOU KNOW BEST FOR ANYONE, INCLUDING YOURSELF -- YOU DON'T!

Day 30

Wow! Nearly a whole month!

There is a force much, much larger than us at work. It seems every success book or successful speaker talks about this in their own way. There seems to be a natural goodness or flow, which always takes us down the best/right path, as long as we don't resist it.

However, I learned that thinking that I (this thinking, rational, reasonable, reality-based self) know best is a true interference with this flow. By thinking, or perhaps over-thinking, I pull myself away from my balance and get all "in my head." This ends up leading me away from my own balance and the resulting flow of what is truly best for me.

I realized that the control I had been holding on to so strongly for decades regarding my business, and my entire life, was actually another form of resistance. I had learned some success from this extreme effort, but I see now that it was actually counter-product-ive. For the amount of energy I put into controlling everything, I didn't get nearly the results I should have. Had I "let go and let God," I would have found that inner balance which would have made every ac-tion I ever took so much more in alignment with the natural success-flow of my life!

By calming my mind, meditating, and trusting that functioning from a balanced stance would bring me insights that I could never have known with only my conscious mind, I ended up allowing the good flow again!

In addition, I found that as soon as I start thinking *I* know best for someone else, I always end up going down some sort of dead-end path. Perhaps I help them a little or short-term, but eventually I end up having to back-track and get back in balance again.

I have learned that I *never* know best for anyone else, either! In fact, I have *no right* to "know best" for them. Not only is it disrespectful, since everyone is their own person and has their own right to their own life, but I end up filling my head with false pride which always leads me astray.

LESSON 53: TAKE CARE OF YOURSELF. IF YOU DON'T, NOBODY ELSE WILL.

Y ou are the only person in this world who can truly care for yourself adequately. You are the only person who can make you happy. You are the only person who can be in harmony and balance with yourself.

Through this bump, I have been sad. *Really* sad! But every time, I ended up angry because I eventually concluded that I was not going to let someone else take away my happiness! My right to happiness is mine, and mine alone! When I allow myself to be sad because of *anything anyone else* does, then I have given this right away! When I realize I have done this without even knowing it, I get angry. I use this anger to reset me back to *owning my own happiness!*

Shortly before my Grandmaster passed away in 2016, I had been struggling with some interpersonal issues about which he and I spoke. As was typical for him to do, he listened very carefully then gave some short, succinct advice. He told me that my life is my responsibility, nobody else's. He said we are born alone and we die alone, and that ultimately everything we do is our own responsibility.

I think he was telling me to stop looking outward to any other person, including him, for my assurance, satisfaction, happiness, contentment, feedback, or confidence. He wanted me to pull it from inside myself and to connect with, and stay connected to, my inner-self so that *no matter what* may happen out in this world, I will *always* be melded with my innerself.

You must care for yourself. Nobody else will! Of course, those that love you will try to do nice things for you. But *nothing* anyone else does for you will be what you really need and eventually this will become clear to you in the form of sadness, anger, or resentment. The reason is that you are looking for harmony with your inner-self and *nobody* else in this whole world can give you that. The more you look and need this from others, the more disappointed you'll be.

Instead, accept this responsibility to care for yourself and do it. Love yourself! Truly, make caring for yourself your number one priority! Only when you have cared for yourself, found peace and happiness with yourself, and stopped burdening others with this need, can you truly be free from the self-inflicted bondage of trying to get from others that which they *cannot* give to you. In addition, you'll stop hurting other people in the process.

I had to dig deep in my own mind to find ways to be happy, through what was turning out to be the worst financial time of my life. I knew I had cash reserves for about another 30 days, but after that, something was going to give. I had fears every few minutes of people coming in to take everything of value from our house, foreclosure of the home mortgage, eviction from our business warehouse (with inventory in it which I would then have *no way* of selling), and my family living homeless or in a manner which would significantly damage my two small growing children.

I started with small things. I worked *incredibly hard* to find things to be happy about. It had initially seemed there was nothing happy in the whole world! But with immense effort, I found happiness. This shift in thinking *allow*ed the beauty and wonder which was all around me to enter my mind. I had to briefly push aside all this sadness and watch carefully for *anything* that might make me happy. Then I had to repeat this over and over, as sad thoughts tried to edge their way back in!

I first found it in my soon-to-be two-year-old son. His innocent, joyful ways make me laugh. I focused intently on him, what it was like to be him. I realized that he had no awareness whatsoever of what was going on all around him, especially in my mind.

Of course, he sensed all wasn't normal, but nonetheless his beautiful spirit kept him thriving and loving every moment of his life as only a two-year-old can do!

I found that the more I enjoyed him, the more I was *able* to enjoy him and everything else! At one point, I spent approximately 30 minutes just entranced by his awesomeness. I imagined times when I was a little child like him, thinking of all that my father and mother must have done and gone through, which I never knew. I imagined that, now as an adult, I was still just a small child like him, and that I could find ways to insulate myself from these circumstances so that deep inside I could find peace.

With practice and a concerted effort to *make times* to find beauty, I was able to find more and more beauty all around me. I found beauty in strangers. I found beauty in the way the light hit the wall in the living room. I found beauty in the way everyone I knew was doing what they knew to do, what they thought was best for their lives. I found beauty in the cycles of nature and the way all life experiences cycles. I found beauty in this bump, just the down-part of one of my cycles of life.

I had written in my diary: "This joy is so good. My whole family is feeling it in me. I want to keep it forever. I know the wind will blow, but I can remain happy through it. Remain calm and loving and peaceful in my mind. No anxiety. Nothing bad. Just continue this momentum of joy. Sense when it wants to change and catch it fast. Recover by eliminating resistance to joy by calm mind, appreciation, meditation or sleep!!"

I saw just how wonderful the effect was of caring for myself. Being happy is the best indicator of your spiritual, mental, and physical health. Caring for myself led me to happiness - There was nothing else that could have happened. Once I was happy, my deep self-care and self-harmony seemed to exude out from me, flowing over every one I came in contact with!

I promised myself that day that *Taking Care of Myself would be my Number One Life Priority!*

LESSON 54:
ONE PLUS ONE
IS THREE.

My wife and I recommitted to getting through this stronger and better than ever. We aggressively started adding new items to our online catalog. I'm so proud that we ended up adding over 1800 new items during this time period! All this hard work will pay its rewards for months and years to come, when we get turned back on again!

Because she and I both entered harmony with ourselves, then aligned with each other, there was some sort of a compounding effect. This was very much like compounding interest, where the money you made on your initial money ends up making you even more money! By aligning on a common goal, with a common intent and shared focus and passion, we were able to do amazing things!

Truly she and I did the work of three, four, five, or even more people by harmonizing! And, it felt great! It felt like we had already succeeded. In fact we had, because we did all we could to affect the current situation in a positive way in a manner we knew would bring substantial results! It was wonderful!

I started analyzing other areas of our life together and realized that *all* the areas in which we were in harmony were booming in magnificent ways! I was so delighted that we were starting to do the same with this business, now!

DAY 31

We spent this Sunday enjoying peaceful, joyful family time, full of laughter and love! I realized the only relevant thing for me to do was to remain in this harmonious, happy place, because the resolution to this situation would come better, faster, and more easily than I ever dreamed, when the only thing I was attracting was joy, peace, and love!

LESSON 55:
MEDITATING
EVERY MORNING
TRULY DOES MAKE
A DIFFERENCE.

I analyzed the days I had meditated recently and the days I hadn't and found that 100% of the time on those days when I started with a ten to twenty minute meditation, something really good came to me in a surprising, unexpected way! So, I decided to meditate every morning!

But no sooner than I made this promise to myself, I stopped meditating. It was like some part of me was saying, "you can't make me!" I was actually defiant to *myself!* This surprised me, because rather than simply not meditate, and start my day as though on auto-pilot, I could actually feel this challenge inside of me.

I tried numerous things to force, convince, and even cajole myself into meditating. *I* knew it was best, but no matter what I did, I just couldn't get myself to do it. As I probed deeper, I felt a feeling of inadequacy, as though by meditating or relying on my inner-self for harmony, *I* was less of a person, less of a man. Hmm... Where did this come from?

LESSON 56: SET YOUR PRIDE ASIDE BY LOVING YOUR LITTLE SELF.

I realized it was that same conditioning I had learned over the past decades, which told me that "putting my nose to the grindstone", was the solution. I didn't want to believe how, seemingly magically, numerous good things sort of just happened to me on the days I meditated. I knew it wasn't magical. It was my subconscious recognizing patterns it had not been looking for before, and prompting me to take action in ways it wouldn't have before. But still I didn't want someone or something else doing it for me. I'm a man and I was going to get through this myself!

So, I tried to put this pride aside, again, forcefully. But the more I tried, the more this other part of me fought back. I could see that this wasn't going to be good, if I continued this approach.

I tried to dig deep into myself to see just why I would have to uphold this strong pride. After much analysis, I concluded that this part of me, likely when I was young, was afraid of not being good enough and was fearful of ridicule, failure, and rejection. So, I imagined giving this little part of myself a big hug and promising him that I would be there with him and not let anyone hurt him.

I know, this sounds silly. I almost didn't write it, but the results were *so amazing* that I just had to share it with you! If you've ever experienced this type of pride or insurrection against yourself, try it. Seriously... give it a try. Close your eyes for 60 seconds and hug your little self, and reassure him/her that you love them and will always protect them.

When I did this, I literally cried. The tears came in waves and they were tears of joy. I felt the wall come down and the idea of meditating seemed like a good idea again, rather than being held as a prisoner-of-war!

LESSON 57: IT'S ALL RELATIVE.

I thought about many things in my business and personal life which I thought were bad before and concluded that they just weren't bad at all, compared to this! So, living in a world of infinites, I applied that logic to this situation, and concluded that it's not the worst either. Not that I wanted to see or experience or even imagine anything worse, but the logic was strong that this wasn't the worst. And if things could get infinitely worse than this, then this isn't even very bad at all. In fact, it's so not-bad, that it truly isn't even bad at all!

So, I applied this concept to many other areas of my life and thinking:

- My mind: I always knew that having a strong mind was a key, but I thought there was only a single indicator of mental strength. I learned that this was only one direction, and relative to it were numerous other directions, all of which I'm discussing in this book.

- My outlook: I had felt that things were generally quite dark and gloomy over the past few years. I realized that relative to this (or other bad times) they really weren't bad at all! There was actually awesomeness all around me, all the time, in all areas of my life!!

- My happiness: I kept looking for things to make me happy. But all the happiness I found never stacked up relative to the perfect, ideal happiness I had been desiring and found in my inner-self!

- My business: I recall complaining, just recently, about how the sales were down and the negative effects of this. Relative to *zero sales* we've had over the past 31 days, *any sales* were great! I decided that I am *never, ever, ever* going to complain about sales being too low. I resolved to always find delightment in every single sale we ever make again!!

- My opportunities: I felt that there was nothing else I could do. I had tried an entirely new venture last year, which I put over 2000 hours in to, and it resulted in $250 of sales! I was disheartened. Relative to no sales at all, even that was a lot. I realized that there are ample opportunities all around me, everywhere!

By seeing my position as relative, rather than absolute, my mind was freed to first see a bigger picture, then to move in the directions of my choosing. When or if you feel you are stuck or trapped in a situation, briefly step out of it and think relatively about just how much, much, much more worse it could be. Then allow this to sling-shot you in the other direction with power and energy like you've never had before!

Day 32

For the third day in a row, I woke up early, at exactly 7:14AM! In my meditation, an inclination came to me that if I were to visualize it flipped it over, where the upside-down "4" looks like the "ch" sound in Cyrillic, 7:14 would mean "chill." Who knows what it really meant, but it felt right and good, so I ran with "chill." I took it as a reminder to chill-out. Relax. Not to take everything so seriously. Enjoy the moment. It seemed helpful.

LESSON 58:
THERE IS A MUCH, MUCH, MUCH BIGGER PICTURE.

I had a thought that we will get turned back on at just the right time. By right, I mean that I am not the only player here. There are numerous people whose lives are involved in and affected by this event. Somehow, I felt 100% confident that the outcome which would come would be exactly right for all of us involved.

In one of the wonderful talks my Father and I have had about the meaning of life, the Universe, and everything, he mentioned the concept of the Infini-verse. Scientists and quantum physicists have shown that we live in a Multi-verse, where there are many possible outcomes to each situation. My Dad's explanation of an Infini-verse was that at any given infinitesimally-small moment there were an infinite number of paths or outcomes, and that all involved in each situation were contributors to the path. As such, every person involved will effectively manifest *their* own version of reality simultaneously in a way that provides each person movement on their own path while perfectly contributing to the paths of everyone else involved.

So, I was able to apply this thinking to my current bump and saw that we are all co-creating this experience. I realized that I was not the only one. Of course, until now, I felt that this was happening *to* me. Today, I got some insight that I had contributed to this result and that its remedy was coming in the best possible way for all involved! Thinking this way truly felt correct and accurate, and deeply healing in some way I couldn't quite understand.

LESSON 59:
YOU'RE STILL HUMAN; CUT YOURSELF SOME SLACK.

But then, somehow all my learning thus far went out the window and I felt despair. Twenty years ago, I had bought life insurance, which, interestingly enough, would have covered every conceivable way of dying. Six months ago, I let it lapse. I felt so, so angry with myself for having done this, because at this moment, I could clearly see another avenue to provide for all those I love.

Looking back on that day, I can see how human I was being at that moment, and feel so incredibly grateful that this bump happened when it did, not six months earlier! I know you're going to read to the end, but I'll give you a hint... This story has a good ending!

So, if you're ever feeling down, so far down that life doesn't seem worth continuing, find something to hang on to, and HANG ON! Hold on for another minute. Then do it again... and again... and again... and again... and again... and again... and again... and again... and again... and again... and again. You just never really know how amazing the future can be, or how wonderfully powerful the moment you're experiencing will seem down the line.

I know... it's hard to understand, believe, or even conceive, but just hold on. Give yourself a break. You're human and suffering is real for humans. But suffering isn't everything. It's only a temporary feeling indicating distance from your ideal-flow!

Day 33

I know... You're thinking today *must* be the day you get turned back on? No... Sadly, NO!

Again, I was woken up early, at 7:09, which turned over would be "BOL," which is a common term in our industry for Bill of Lading used in freight transportation. I took this as a clue that we would be shipping things again soon!

LESSON 60: ACCEPTING THAT WHICH YOU DON'T LIKE IS LIBERATING.

So, unlike the past few days, I immediately went online, fully expecting to see that we were turned back on. We weren't and I got sad, really sad. I spent the whole day getting my mind back to positive, where I could be ok with anything that happened. I wasn't ok, but somehow I had to be. What choice did I have?

Seriously, what choice did I have? It was what it was. Yeah, I didn't like it but, so what?! Today, I learned acceptance at an even deeper level. I reminded myself of all the good I had, which I would continue to have *no matter what happened.* I reminded myself to just go with it! Stop resisting. Accept that which is, without any regard to my feelings about it.

By doing this, I later learned that I freed myself from the actual situation! By accepting it, I was able to stop fighting it over and over and over, in my mind! This freed me to begin thinking "out of the box" about the situation. Ironically, accepting what-was allowed me to let go of what-was so I could begin seeing what-was-to-be!

LESSON 61: YOU ARE A GOOD PERSON.

You are a good person. Really, you are. How do I know? I just know. You were born good. You were born amazing! You were born as pure love! Every baby is. Every single one, without exception! I truly believe this!

So you may have gone down a "bad" or "wrong" or "different" path. But it's not too late. Seriously, please try closing your eyes now and asking yourself: Are you really a good person? Yes - I thought so! Do you mean harm to others? Of course not - I know! Are you caring and good? Do you do your best? Do you care so much that it hurts sometimes? Do you desperately want to do good in your life?

Nobody does anything without a reason that makes sense to them. Read that again. Inside their mind, they behave in whatever way they believe is best. If it doesn't seem best to you, me, or the whole world, simply means we aren't using the same logic they are using. But they *are* using logic and reason for their behavior, even if it's just conditioning they learned as a small child.

Does this mean they are bad? NO! I'm not saying bad behavior isn't bad - of course it is and I'm certainly not, in any way, condoning bad behavior. I'm simply asking you to understand that *you* are not bad! Nothing you've done has been ill-intended. It all made sense to you at that time. Accepting this will free you to grow, add new logic to your reasoning, and become more of the person you deeply desire to become.

Consuming yourself with thinking you're bad not only reinforces the neural pathways of bad-ness, but locks you in your own mental prison cell where you are your own accuser, judge, jury, and warden. Then, you become your own executioner, slowly killing yourself daily in little, destructive ways.

Start today, right now, by accepting that you *ARE* good, inherently, and that all you have ever done has been the *best you possibly could have done at that moment with the experiences and knowledge you had at that time!* This acceptance will liberate you in ways you can't even imagine right now.

How do I know all this? Today, on Day 33, I struggled even more deeply than I ever have with my own good-ness, or perceived lack thereof. I realized that I am a good person! I have always known this! I am loving and caring and good! I always help people! I am sensitive and kind and good! This actually matters, nearly more than anything else in my life!

All night long, I had incredibly vivid dreams of sales *pouring in*, more than ever before!! It was so wonderful!!!

Day 34

I was woken up at 7:10 today, which turned over is "OIL," which I took to mean I needed to get a massage and care for myself. I didn't get the massage (couldn't justify a penny on myself, still), but I did care for myself today.

I took some time to go out and drive around, to clear my mind. It felt good. I ended up in the parking lot of a mall and just sat there. I started feeling disregarded by people from my life, whom I used to spend much time with but as of the past few years, have hardly seen. It was getting so sad, so I caught it, realized it wasn't good for me to think, and let it go! Yay!

Today is the day before Thanksgiving and I recalled thinking that how, during my years in retail just before major holidays, the strangest people would come out. I was realizing I was now one of those strange people! Hah! LOL!

My mind kept taking me back to past times in my life, which weren't very good. So much blame had been put on me and I still, all these years later, was struggling with guilt because I had heard how I was to blame so many times. I had actually started believing it. I was literally yelling at myself in my head that I WAS NOT TO BLAME!! I guess it helped because I really don't like this type of thinking anyway.

LESSON 62: THE END IS RARELY EVER ACTUALLY THE END.

I learned today that even though I feel like I can't do it any more, I can. I learned that I can do it. I know I can! I know I can be strong! I'm just so tired of being strong! I want a rest for a little while. Then I can be strong again. This is ok. I just needed to take care of myself. That was my only job now.

Day 35

It's Thanksgiving! Starting to wonder if we'll get turned back on by Cyber Monday or not?

But I sensed and caught the negative loop that was forming, and got my mind back positive again. I realized everything will be ok, somehow. It will be ok... Somehow it already was. Nothing was nearly as bad as it felt yesterday. Somehow things will be even better than I ever dreamed! I reminded myself that I am good and I attract good to me.

Last night I dreamed of reconciling with people from my past and recovering things which had been important to me but were taken from me.

I spent the day with family and hardly thought of the business situation at all!! I had bought a cheap guitar earlier this year and picked it up today and tried to start learning how to play it a little. It was so fun!

LESSON 63:
YOUR MIND IS
YOUR OWN.

I realized that my mind was so much clearer today in so many ways and that last night was the first night in over a year that I didn't take any medicine for sleeping! So I considered not taking it as often or maybe to stop altogether. I thought that maybe it was actually making me anxious which certainly doesn't help me or the situation at all!

As I thought more about it, I decided to stop altogether! I wanted my mind to be my own, not under the effect of medicine. I slept so well last night without it, and I can again. If I end up waking up early and not being able to sleep, maybe that would be my inner-self encouraging me to go do something, so I would.

By the way, I did stop that day and now, months later as I write this, am so delighted to have such a clearer mind! Your mind is your own! Don't give it away to anyone or anything which might have a negative effect upon it! Enjoy the feelings, both happy and sad. Embrace the suffering, and rejoice in the wonder! Life your life - every moment of it, entirely yours!

Day 36

I was woken up at 7:07 both today and yesterday. Turned over, this is "LOL," as in Laugh-Out-Loud. I took this to mean the Universe was laughing, more like chuckling over me, this life of mine, and just how seriously I was taking this situation.

LESSON 64: A VICTIM MENTALITY MAKES YOU THE VICTIM.

I realized today that while I am not a victim, I did bring this whole event into my life with a victim mentality. As mentioned prior, there were many ways in which I thought I had been wronged, grieved, or even abused, in my life and especially over the past year. I learned that thinking this way made me behave in a victim-manner, which essentially encouraged people to treat me as such.

In addition, most importantly, it kept me from doing those things I needed to do to ensure I was not a victim. I had nearly entirely stopped performing regular maintenance, in all areas of my life, both personal and business. Had I taken the necessary steps months ago, to ensure we were under no risk of attacks such as this intellectual property claim which caused all this, we wouldn't be in this situation. My victim-mentality made me the victim, literally!

Having learned that you can't focus on something you don't want and expect it to be gone, I instead created a replacement for it. My replacement, while not perfect, was that "I am a champion." I installed this over and over in my mind and it started to take root and replace my old victim-mentality!

An hour later, I was already behaving differently! Last night, my Prius started blinking the tire light, meaning the air was low in a tire. I had planned to try to get to the dealership sometime next week, which likely would have meant something more like two-plus weeks! Instead, I just went and did it on the way to where I was going. It was done and I felt so good. Who knows - maybe I averted a significant issue by performing this maintenance! I'm so glad I learned this lesson! I finally got it!!

As the day went on, I could see so clearly the many issues that I had been thinking of ten, 25, even 50 times a day, where I was feeling victimized by someone.

For example, a very close friend of mine for the past few years suddenly and without warning, nine months ago, just said that she didn't want to talk any more until further notice. Not having heard anything from her yet, I kept wondering what I had done wrong, what I should have done, what I didn't do, and what was wrong with me to make her do this.

After fixing my victim-mentality, I realized just

how much a victim I had made myself in that situation and decided she was simply doing what was best for her. Whether it had anything to do with me or not, it was what she concluded was best.

I was not a victim in any way. I concluded that I can never allow myself be a victim again!

I started running this mantra in my mind: "This is my life and I love it! I am victim to nobody and nothing! I am my own champion!"

Day 37

Today was the last day of November and I never thought that after 37 we still wouldn't be turned on. In addition to my regular work, I was now spending an extra five-plus hours a day, seven days a week, just juggling money, applying for loans, completing financial statements, robbing Peter to pay Paul, meeting with vendors, trying so hard to help my employees whose hours I had to cut to zero now, and doing all I could to be ready to boom at moment's notice still hoping to be turned on in time for the holiday season.

To give you perspective, the time period from Cyber Monday to Dec 23 typically generated 50% of our annual revenue and 90% of our annual profit! And, we were so heavily stocked (all purchased with debt) with holiday-type of items, that if it didn't sell by Dec 25, we would be forced to clearance-price it so much that we would actually not even get enough to pay back the loans for the price we paid on it!

LESSON 65:
ALLOW YOURSELF
TO SEE IT AS
IT CAN BE.

I tried doing a visualization today during my meditation, where I imagined my warehouse covered by a black shroud which was blocking all the energy flow. Then, in my mind, I just opened it up from the top and allowed a beautiful energy to flow down into it! It traveled down through all the products to our employees, vendors, carriers, and distribution centers, then into the customers themselves. Everyone was so deeply nourished by this flow. It was just wonderful! I clung to the memory of that visualization many times, in the coming weeks!

LESSON 66: CALM YOUR MIND, AND THEN ALLOW THE ANSWER TO COME TO YOU.

I learned during the meditation and visualization, that all I had to do was get started. Then it just flowed on its own and was wonderful! I knew I wasn't making it up or thinking it. It was more like watching a movie. Amazingly, it wasn't hard. I just got out of the way, stopped thinking, and let it flow!

A self-help video I heard today on YouTube said, "If you're not hearing a *strong* YES, then it is a NO". That means that when you're meditating regularly, your subconscious will continue to show you over and over in strong ways that which is your best path.

If you have to think about it too much, weigh the pros and cons, or try hard to figure out if it's the right course of action, then it isn't! The right course of action will come to you clearly. In the beginning, you might not know how to hear it, but little by little you'll get better at sensing it. Eventually, it will be very clear. I'm getting ahead of myself, but I feel you should know that the ultimate remedy to this bump had been something I had stumbled across a few times before I recognized it as a viable option.

So, I thought back on my life. There were *many* things I did out of obligation, threat of loss, or social pressure, for which I hadn't actually heard a strong "yes." In all those cases, it didn't work out well for me or anyone else involved. Looking back, in all those cases, I would have been much better saying "no" than going along with what someone else wanted. But at the time, I thought I was doing the best thing! Now I see differently!

I also saw many things, mostly in recent years, where there was clearly a strong "yes." In *all* of these cases, it was so clearly right!

My wife and I took a much-need reprieve and went to a Led Zeppelin tribute band concert tonight, which was truly exactly the break we needed from all this!

Day 38

Today is Dec 1 and tomorrow is Cyber Monday! I'm mildly hopeful that we'll get turned back on today or tomorrow, but no longer highly optimistic after 38 days! My lost sales are now approximately 20% of the entire holiday! So, I really needed to be back on by

Cyber Monday!

LESSON 67: TRUST YOUR GUT FEELING.

I started the day with a meditation. Interestingly enough, I sat down with the prominent owner of the marketplace facilitator/fulfillment provider, in my meditation! It was sort of like he came to me. He said he saw and understood my heart, and apologized for things his company had implemented that were intended to improve things, causing trouble sometimes. He seemed so sincere and honest. I had always admired him, and refused to believe that he was an evil or ill-intentioned person as recent media has made him out to be.

I have no idea if I was just making this up in my mind or if somehow we actually did communicate telepathically, but in either case I now have a strong feeling of positive toward him and the whole company. My gut feeling was that they weren't really trying to cause trouble for people, but instead balancing priorities, which likely included threats or other legal concerns at such high levels, perhaps from other countries even, that I know nothing about.

It seemed odd to me that I now had heard three

stories from other sellers who had been turned off around the same time, just before the holidays, this year and last. But I reasoned that perhaps they were getting ready for the busy season and didn't have time for any diversions, so it made more sense for them to crack-down hard in October, just to be sure all would be fine in November and December.

LESSON 68: A POSITIVE OUTLOOK LEADS TO OPPORTUNITIES AND SOLUTIONS.

I t didn't feel right to me to have negative feelings toward them. I have always appreciated the opportunity and services they provide me. Trusting my gut feeling, that they are good and trying to do good, really helped me tremendously. It didn't change anything outside myself, but it did program my subconscious mind to identify with opportunities and solutions, rather than seeing issues and problems.

Of course, I don't suspect I would have learned this lesson had it not felt like I had an actual conversation during my meditation. Had I not meditated, I am certain that seeing the positive would have been entirely impossible for me at this time. But during the mediation, my mind was open to things other than this-reality. Somehow, the positive from it snuck into my subconscious mind in ways it never would have in a fully conscious state-of-mind.

During the meditation, I saw sparks flying down through my warehouse flowing out to our products, customers, marketplace, money, people, and even some of my most exciting dreams! It was as though there was an energy flowing through everyone, providing abundance and goodness.

Throughout the day, I found my mind imagining that now I was in the place I had been a few years ago, when I had money in the bank and no debt, with substantial annual sales! What would I do? If that were the current case, I would just pay the rent and continue to pay my employees their regular pay to make the warehouse perfect for whatever came next.

LESSON 69:
NEVER TAKE
GOOD PEOPLE
FOR-GRANTED.

I have the most wonderful employees in the world! As it became clear to me a couple weeks back that I had absolutely no clear idea of when we would be turned back on, I began cutting every possible expense in the company... Phone lines, fax numbers, phone system options, hosting plans, domain names, reprogramming thermostats, canceling maintenance contracts, discontinuing wireless service, insurance, etc., etc., etc.

Included in this was cutting employees, which was the last thing I did. My team is made up of the most wonderful people you have ever known! They not only had completely understood and agreed to take significant cuts in their hours, but two of them who had loaned me money just prior to this to purchase additional holiday product, agreed to postpone repayment until spring! Oh my, I knew I was blessed!

I hope someday I can make it up to them! This

wasn't their risk! They didn't sign-up to be business owners. They want to come in, do their work, go home, and get a paycheck. I felt horrible cutting their hours so low, but I had no other choice. I had already cut my pay to zero, drained my personal savings, and sold all the stock in my retirement account, just to keep the doors open. So, I did what I had to do, but I will never forget the beautiful gift they gave me by being so incredibly understanding. I only hope I can repay them many times over, in the coming years!

Day 40

Day 40... Day 40... DAY FORTY!!! HOLY COW!! How did 40 days pass already? What is going on here? Cyber Monday came and went and now we're deep in the holiday season. We only have approximately twelve more good selling days left. But MAYBE we'll get turned on... This is what I was thinking on Day 40!!

LESSON 70: FOCUS ON THE SOLUTION.

I decided to drill down in my mind to see if I could come up with any possible solutions, which might have been right here but I wasn't seeing. Of course, since my mind had been consumed with the negative of this situation, it seemed reasonable that I must have missed something. What solution? ANY solution! ALL solutions! Anything that even resembled a solution! I pushed my mind to focus on it. A LOT!!

I considered selling into the European Union... That had been something I was considering for 2020, so maybe I should move it up and do it now? Maybe some side business? Or something software-related, from my past? Maybe even play my (really novice) guitar music? Write my own music?

I decided that I needed *anything* which would move me forward in the direction I wanted to go in life, both specifically regarding this situation and generally related to what I wanted out of life. By doing this, it seemed I would resonate with those outcomes and not with the problem.

I realized that this is the approach I had always used before! But somehow this bump had set me back into some negative slump, from which I sensed I was somehow emerging!

LESSON 71: LIFE IS LIKE A BANK. YOU CAN DEPOSIT IN ONE BRANCH AND WITHDRAW FROM ANOTHER.

Years ago, I had been a sales manager. I used to explain to my trainees that life is like a large bank. You can deposit in one location and withdraw from another. I would explain that if you put the energy into one customer or lead that didn't result in a sale, you would still be able to withdraw later and elsewhere from that effort.

I didn't have a reason for this, other than it seemed to be true 100% of the time. Case after case after case, my team would tell me stories of how it was true. Perhaps what made it true was that their minds never went negative when they didn't get a sale. In fact, they got more excited and even expected the next one!

So, I decided to take that approach here. I saw that I could put my actions and efforts into nearly any endeavor which seemed reasonably likely to produce financial results at this point and if it didn't, the effort was being deposited into the bank and I would one day withdraw it (hopefully with substantial interest, too!)

LESSON 72: NEVER COMPLAIN.

I felt like I had finally reached some understanding about what to do. Prior to this, I kept asking myself what I was supposed to do and why this happened to me. I was just grasping at straws but never got an answer! Apparently, I was asking the wrong questions.

I see now that those questions presumed victim mentality, as we discussed before. But now, I knew I would move forward strongly and confidently in whatever direction seemed best at that time, and I could expect results to come one way or another!

I realized that while I wasn't explicitly complaining to anyone about this, I was complaining to myself. By listening to the voice in my head that had been wallowing all through this bump, I wasn't looking at the solution.

So, I promised myself that day, to never, ever again complain about this situation to anyone, especially myself! Even, all through writing this book, I have tried to only point out the most basic, necessary, and relevant facts in order that you can have enough context to draw the appropriate contrast from the event and its related stories.

I concluded that never does complaining help. In fact, just the act of saying negative things tells yourself that they're true. Perhaps you were speculating or analyzing a situation. As soon as you say (even in your own mind) that they are truly negative, which in effect is a complaint, you believe it. From then on, you're now spending energy just to stop going negative, and have very little left to even move positively. So, don't ever complain!

LESSON 73: YOU CAN'T THINK TWO OPPOSITIONAL THOUGHTS AT THE SAME TIME.

My rational mind has been consumed with doom, gloom, and failure thinking. Now, I had replaced that with confidence that I could identify and work toward a solution, with the full expectation of results.

I couldn't have simply changed my mind through will-power, because the negative had taken root. Instead, I had to consciously replace it. The key to that, for me, was meditating. It forced my mind to suspend the negative just long enough to slip in some positive mental movies. As I chose to believe these, as though they were real and had actually happened, they began to replace the negative. At the time, I wasn't even aware this was happening. I was just happy to feel happier again.

Some sort of energetic momentum was now

underway. The positive started getting easier to connect with and I found myself even thinking of positive things on my own during the day without even trying!

I recall feeling that this was no big deal and would somehow work itself out! I then started seeing many examples of my past, where things seemed big and insurmountable and how they had always, 100% of the time, worked themselves out in ways I could have never dreamed!

My journal for this day said: "There are infinite realities. So there are infinite moments, each of which has infinite paths. So it is entirely possible for me to choose the one which gives me everything I want while in NO way infringing on anything anyone else wants! Just allow it to flow and there I am." This was another insight of the Infini-verse I had explained prior. What a happy, successfully confident way to see the world!

LESSON 74: PUT BIG THINGS INTO PERSPECTIVE.

I decided to put this whole event into financial perspective, to try to understand where we fit, in the big picture. So I calculated the numbers and realized that if the miles spent driving to my Taekwondo School, which takes about 20 minutes, were the annual revenue of the marketplace facilitator, our annual revenue last year would be just nine inches of that path! Not even a single step... Not even the length of my shoe!!

I felt grateful for having even been associated with them for the past decade! I appreciated the opportunity they gave me to work with them, and all the wonderful things it afforded me in my life for so many years!

I realized that I had eleven years selling on their platform, which was 121 months. Two months down really isn't much. This perspective helped me!

LESSON 75: YOU'RE NOT REALLY AS IMPORTANT AS YOU THINK YOU ARE.

This really helped me realize that nothing was being done to me. All I had worked for over the past 20 years to build this business was truly inconsequential, nothing whatsoever, to the marketplace facilitator! This realization was liberating and truly freed me to stop feeling self-important and get on with whatever action I was going to take next!

LESSON 76: WHEN THINGS GET CLOGGED, CLEAN THEM, LET THEM SIT, AND ALLOW THEM TO FLOW AGAIN.

We had our first big snow storm of the year. In fact, it rained, then snowed on the rain, then iced on top of that, leaving a real mess. There was no way I could have driven out of our driveway. So I went to fire up our snow blower and it would not start. For hours, I tinkered with it and concluded that I must have forgotten to run the zero-octane gas through it in the spring last year. So, I eventually called and scheduled an appointment for them to come pick it up to repair it, the soonest of which would be nearly a week later. I then spent six-plus hours breaking apart ice and shoveling what

I could since we had to get to appointments the following day.

I was so frustrated at first, because it seemed everything just kept going wrong even though I kept doing good things. After I came in from shoveling, it occurred to me that the gas line of the snow blower was very much like our cash flow. It was a flow that had gotten clogged. So, I had cleaned it the best I could and let it sit, knowing things like this have a way of working themselves out when you do all you can to help.

The next day, it snowed again and I decided to try the snow blower. It started first try! This was so confirming for me that great things were going to come.

LESSON 77: PREVENTATIVE MAINTENANCE IS WORTH 10X, 100X, EVEN 1000X ITS COST.

I realized that, had I spent the five minutes and 5 dollars pouring in the spring gas before storing the snow blower, I would have saved eight-plus hours and potentially a $500 repair. This is an incredible return on investment! I really had to let this sink in, and try to apply it to all areas of my life. Of course I had done it in past years, but for some reason I hadn't this time.

I applied this lesson to my business bump and realized that had I put in place proper preventative procedures and policies, and enforced them, we would have never been in this situation because we would have either replied faster to the IP claimant, or not even allowed ourselves to be in a situation where he could have thought we were violating his IP on his on-line listing.

The problem was that I didn't know there was even a potential problem. I completely and entirely missed the risk. I didn't know the risk even existed, nor did I ever dream it could have impeded my business like it did!

This lesson is really big! Take a moment now and think about your business, job, or life, and see what areas of it could really take you to your knees. What potential problem could occur, typically in a short amount of time from an external influence that could change everything about the way you are living your life right now? Then, see if there is *any*thing you can do, now, to mitigate that risk. How can you most likely move yourself out harm's way and keep yourself safe?

This reminds me of car maintenance. When I was 16, I got my first car, a 1976 Chevrolet Chevette, with a 1.4L engine, no power steering, no power brakes, and a head-gasket problem that consumed oil nearly as much as it did gas! My father told me that the two areas to never avoid maintenance on were tires and brakes, because if your tires or breaks fail and you're on the highway at 65 MPH, there is a good chance your life will end. A relatively small investment of new tires and brakes has the greatest chance of saving your life. Sure there are other critical elements of the car, but those two have the greatest potential of killing you, should they fail.

My dad's lesson really stuck with me about cars. I wish I had understood the same about my business. But I did now and I vowed to always take the necessary time to look for hidden risks and address all potential areas which could drive the business to its knees.

Day 41

Today was a day of reflection:

- I recalled that I was projecting "lack" so I got "lack."

- I dug up an old affirmation/mantra I had used 15 years ago: "I am so happy and grateful now that money is coming to me in increasing quantities from multiple sources!" and started repeating it over and over and over in my head, until I actually started feeling happy about it!

LESSON 78: PEOPLE DO WHAT MAKES SENSE FOR THEM, WITHOUT REGARD TO YOU.

I felt stronger now than ever that I refused to believe anyone was "out to get me" in this bump. I realized that feeling this way is inherently *my* way of looking at the world. Being an optimist has gotten me in trouble before, but it is who I am and I realized that it was time to honor myself and believe that nobody is or ever has really tried to screw me over.

Sure, I've been hurt, badly! But I believe those who hurt me always did what they did for reasons that made sense for them, with little regard for me, either positively or negatively. I had gotten off-track regarding this type of thinking for many years, but now I was back! By believing this again, I freed myself from even allowing a victim mentality into my mind. It was impossible because nobody could ever intend on hurting me without it somehow making sense to them. This somehow made it alright in my mind, or at least liberated me.

I haven't taken sleep medicine in over a week now and my head is incredibly clear and I'm sleeping very well!

LESSON 79: TAKE CARE OF THE PEOPLE AND THINGS THAT YOU VALUE.

Day 42

I realized today that this entire experience is truly teaching me so much. But perhaps the largest lesson at the moment is to take care of the people and things that are important to me!

For instance, had I properly taken care of the snow blower in the spring, it would have worked fine in the winter. But I neglected to, for whatever reason, and I paid the price. It makes me think of the saying, "An ounce of prevention is worth a pound of cure." This is so true! I'm applying this to my seller account with the marketplace facilitator, my house, my kids, my wife, my friendships, my students, everyone.

I think I do pretty well with this, regarding people. But I have to do better with things. Regular maintenance is important! I need to do it! I do it with my cars, now I need to do it with everything, including *my business!*

My business won't just run itself! I need to regularly assess all areas, especially those I haven't looked at in a while, and take "care" of them, performing "regular maintenance!" This is a very special business, especially to me! I need to treat it as such!!

Please read that again... If you own a business or have a job, try seeing just how special it is to you, and work on ways to ensure you are treating it as such, on a daily basis! You never know when it can disappear! I do! *Take care of it!*

I learned the hard way that *I need to stay involved with everything that is important to me!* I hope you can learn from my mistake, today, right now, and find something you care about but have been neglecting, and give it some attention, love, or care! Do it *now!*

I got a really powerful insight on day 42... This situation isn't like I have personal debt from indulging in an irresponsible life. I live very frugally and watch my every expense meticulously! All my debt is business debt from a well-planned and conceived business, which is still very bright and successful!

Somehow this really helped me see that as bad as I was feeling about all this, if I were to lose it all due to being unable to repay my debts, I could hold my head high, knowing I made sound business decisions, taking reasonable risks. Of course I am responsible for it, but I need not blame myself. Any such blame would simply be counter-productive at this point.

I had another wonderful meditation today and I saw my Taekwondo teacher, who seemed to tell me:

1. It's ok. It's ok. It is truly all ok!!!

2. Relax. If I get uptight, I will get hurt or hurt myself.

3. Tomorrow is not now. Now is now. Tomorrow is tomorrow. Don't spend any of my precious now on tomorrow. Spend now on now.

These seem so obvious, but that was his way. He was always simple, succinct, and profound!

The third one really hit me, so I'm going to call it out here as another lesson!

LESSON 80: TOMORROW IS NOT NOW. NOW IS NOW. TOMORROW IS TOMORROW. DON'T SPEND ANY OF YOUR PRECIOUS NOW ON TOMORROW. SPEND NOW ON NOW.

Please re-read this again a few times. It's so simple that it almost sneaks into your mind without any mental challenge. But it's also so powerful that this one lesson has the power to change your life!

LESSON 81: BE 100% HAPPY WITH WHAT YOU HAVE WHILE 100% STRIVING FOR MORE.

Here on day 42, I would have been happy to have ANY sales coming. I recall the past, where I always wanted more, bigger, better, faster, and more efficient. It was never enough for me. So I manifested "Not enough" for myself! Hah!

I thought that striving for more was mutually exclusive with being happy with what I had. Now I have learned that I can (and must) be entirely, wholly content with just where I am now. After all, it *is* where I am! What's the sense in not enjoying this moment!

While being fully delighted with exactly where I am now, I must be completely striving for more. Being human means striving for more. This is one of the primary differences between humans and animals. Animals have a top-limit on their achievement. Humans can become and grow more every day, without any limits. In fact, we rebel against any limits on our growth and freedom. This is inherent within us!

So, if you're choosing one or the other, try choosing *both!* Graciously and joyfully appreciate exactly where you are and what you have, while simultaneously expanding, growing, and creating more!

Day 43

Today was my son's two-year birthday! My wife and I did a really good job giving him a spectacular day. With everything money-related completely suspended, we didn't throw him a party, but we did take him to the local children's museum for the first time and he truly had a blast!

I found myself thinking of my father again, wondering what business stresses, fears, and turmoil he was facing on my second birthday. What about my mom? Was she feeling overwhelmed, juggling full-time work, helping my dad, and dealing with me? I realized that all they were dealing with didn't affect my life at all because they saw to that! Just feeling their love was all I needed. The same is true with my son. This really put a lot into perspective!

I had a dream tonight about a business I apparently had forgotten I owned! It was bustling with activity but desperately needing leadership. It was hiring employees like crazy. I recalled thinking it was broke but it was actually pouring in the money! This dream was like some sort of hidden memory! I couldn't recall anything about it but I knew it was my business. I realized that I had let it go and hadn't managed it well, yet somehow it was still good and strong! Then I was on a stage ready to give a speech to 100s of employees. Their faces projected excitement, expectation, and a deep need of whatever I was going to say! I really got excited about it!

Day 44

Still not turned on! YET!! Nearly one week after Cyber Monday and only about one week left of potential holiday sales. I had no idea where I was going with my entire life!

I ran into a school friend of mine from decades ago! We hadn't seen each other for years, but felt instant connection again! She told me how meaningful my ways were back then, which was truly surprising to me, as I didn't think anyone noticed me at all, certainly in not all the ways I had always tried to help people. This was so meaningful! Somehow I needed this!

LESSON 82:
PUT YOURSELF
IN THE OTHER
PERSON'S SHOES.

D ay 45
I decided to really try to think about this from the marketplace facilitator's point of view. How would I feel if I were them? If I had gotten a complaint that one of my sellers violated intellectual property laws, what choice would I have but to take severe action, to not only ensure proper respect and treatment of the laws, but to try to teach my seller a lesson.

Somehow, this helped. It softened and warmed the stark cold reality I was facing. It helped me make this about "just business," and not anything personal.

LESSON 83:
A STRONG FOUNDATION WILL WEATHER MANY STORMS.

I "spoke" with my Taekwondo Grandmaster again. This time, he told me:

1. First things first. Know what's important. Focus upon it and do it. Clear everything else from view.

2. Rest your mind. Don't keep stimulating it. Give it time to rest in order to gain/remain in harmony with yourself.

3. Like a tree survives the external struggle of each winter, it is just fine because it is strong inside. You are strong inside and will be just fine.

I learned that decades of building internal fortitude truly gave me the foundation to weather this storm. In no way was I going to come out of this destroyed. I might be beat up, bruised, tired, and weary, but I'll be fine! I'll shine again, like never before!

If you're going through something difficult now, think of all your past struggles and realize that they fortified an incredibly strong foundation upon which you are now securely hunkered-down during this storm. You'll make it through! The storm will end and the sun will shine again!!

LESSON 84: BEING A GOOD PERSON MATTERS.

Day 46

I have always strongly believed that being a good person matters. Therefore it does, to me, at least! In fact, it matters more than anything else. It is the most critical element in any relationship. By being good, doing what you know in your gut to be right, and treating other people as you would like to be treated, you are thereby allowed to see the best in the other person. This will then result in beautiful harmony, co-creation, and love with everyone with whom you come in contact!

LESSON 85: ALWAYS WORK TO GIVE MORE THAN YOU GET.

I n every interaction, especially business-related, try to give more value to those with whom you're interacting than you will get. Find something extra you can do or give. It might take you a moment, but it might mean the world to the other person. Go out of your way, even just a little, to ensure that they got a better deal than you did.

Don't worry about getting "taken for a ride!" If you are, go for the ride and enjoy it! Instead, try to always tip the scales in the favor of the other. If you do this with every single transaction, you can't help but benefit in the long run. But don't even do it for this reason. Do it, just because it's right and good, and the way you would want to be treated.

Seriously, try this. Tomorrow, make *every* interaction better for the other guy than for you, and in a seemingly magical way, you'll be deeply amazed at what a wonderful day it will be!! Take the challenge and try it!

LESSON 86: FOCUS IS THE KEY.

Day 49

By focusing your mind on what which you desire or are working towards, you are actually molding the energy of life. You are creating something new out of an energetic potential.

Don't focus, for a single moment, on what you don't want. Doing this only molds your life energy into more of what you don't want!

Instead, focus on your own energy and success! This is the juice of life. Ask yourself: What's next? What can I do now? What's the next step to move me closer to my goals? Then, literally, go as fast as you can! Make your life an exhilarating experience!

I'm realizing all this time, these 49 days, have given me ample time to focus! Before, I was scattered, diluting my life energy in too many directions, many of which weren't effective. But I couldn't see this. Now, I can see it! I can understand now that which I want in life and that which I don't! This time taught me to learn about myself, and to listen and care for myself!

One way of focusing is to ensure you are not splitting your energy. Be careful not to allow your mind to think of the "good" of a topic, then the "bad" of the same topic. By doing so, you end up wasting energy and time, and exhausting yourself, ending up back in the same place. In addition, you never allow that all-powerful big momentum to build. Catch yourself early and ensure you never split your energy.

LESSON 87: HEALING IS AUTOMATIC, IF YOU ALLOW IT.

I had been working out hard on a heavy bag and accidentally injured my knuckles, badly. I knew they would heal. I wasn't the slightest bit worried. Sure, they hurt. I couldn't deny the pain, but I didn't focus on it. I just knew healing would come. Like all of us, I have had my share of scrapes, bumps, and bruises. They all have healed. Healing is natural, automatic.

I realized that this lesson applies, not only to my physical body, but to all of life, including this bump! I understood that it will heal itself, in ways that I truly don't, can't, and never will understand. Yet, just like my body, as long as I don't interfere in the healing, it will heal!

Like my knuckles, the pain I am feeling from this bump is teaching me to not do it again!

As I went to bed, I noticed the moonlight coming in the windows of my living room, and it appeared in such a unique way, as though I had never seen it before! I felt such deep appreciation for living in a nice, safe, and comfortable home!

Today was the first day that I referred to this situation as a "bump!"

Day 50

I woke up at 7:07 again! "LOL!" I actually laughed out loud about this! It really is funny! It taught me that from a non-physical, eternal point-of-view, this whole bump is truly not a big deal! There is absolutely nothing to be concerned with for even one second! There are trillions of stars, billions of galaxies, and our little star is one of the smallest.

If our solar system were to disappear, nobody in the entire universe would even notice. So many billions and billions of people are alive right now on Earth and countless billions of others have lived and died here. I am just one of them! I am hardly anything! This perspective reminded me again just how unimportant I am. How refreshing this is, to help me release all stress, anxiety, and worry regarding this bump.

LESSON 88:
LIFE IS GOOD
AND BEAUTY
ABOUNDS.

This life is so good. As I looked around today, I found beauty everywhere. It seemed everything I looked at was beautiful! I saw so much good in people and nature. I felt such deep joy! I saw so many wonderful people, truly amazing people, who were all doing their best to live good lives. I felt so much happiness and learned today that life is really very, very good!

Day 51

Today was a hard day. I really slid back and it felt like I hadn't learned a single thing. None of my lessons were in the forefront of my mind and everything seemed hopeless!

I found my mind feeling cynical about my marketplace facilitator. I was questioning their motives and my logical mind was finding all sorts of ways that they orchestrated this against me and others like me for their gain and our loss. My mind found similarities between what they were doing and some of my past employers.

LESSON 89: THERE ARE THINGS IN LIFE YOU WILL NEVER UNDERSTAND.

I struggled so deeply with trying to understand exactly why and how this was all happening. I just couldn't figure out what I was supposed to do now, or why this was happening to me. Somehow, I caught this negative slide and was able to remind myself that somehow it was all ok and that it wasn't helpful to get mad at myself. This helped a little.

LESSON 90:
WHEN IT'S RIGHT,
EVERYTHING
JUST FALLS
INTO PLACE.

I spent a lot of time today thinking about what I really valued. I asked myself some hard questions and came to some surprising conclusions. I saw a pattern in my life that when it was "right", everything just fell into place. When it was "wrong", it felt like I had to force, wiggle, push, cajole, and ram everything into place, and it never really fit but ended up being a big mess!

I recalled weeks and months before this happened, having little impulses (about half of which I overrode) which, looking back, would have been really good had I honored them. I'm not saying I'm psychic or anything, just that my sub-conscious definitely saw some sort of writing on the wall that I was mostly clueless about. Some things just weren't falling into place and instead of releasing them and flowing around them, I kept trying to make them work.

Each time, of course, they wouldn't and resisted me even more, and yet I kept pushing harder and harder.

Oh, how I wish I had learned to trust that when it's right it will just flow, like magic. There was a lot that was wrong over that past three years with my business, and I didn't address them appropriately by making necessary, even painful, changes. Instead I just kept hoping, trying, and forcing them to work. Guess who lost? Yes, it was me. I have always told my children that when you fight with the truth, the truth will always win. Remember that lesson? I should have heeded my own lesson!

I decided to go away again tomorrow, to take a single night away, to clear my mind and free myself from this situation. Often when I go to a new place, see new things, and experience new events, my mind clears. Last time I went away, somehow things flowed a bit.

I finished the day consciously working to reposition all sorts of recent events in my life such that I could see positive in them. It seemed to work.

As I went to bed, I was able to have total 100% expectation of successful selling again and awesome success, all debts paid, and enjoying a retirement lifestyle with more than enough money coming in. I had 0% resistance to this because I actually had evidence of it: my largest short-term loan was at an all-time low; I had a great plan to pay all other loans; we had some truly great deals with our vendors; of course, we have an amazing staff; and I have a super support system in my life. I realized that I had 100% expectation and 0% resistance, which means it's already a done deal!

Day 52

I woke to receiving three different utility shut-off notices which my warehouse sent to me, and my son had a gigantic "two-year" tantrum for over an hour. This was entirely 180 degrees opposite of what I needed. I told myself I would overcome and get through it. I found respite in the fact that at least thoughts of surrendering to this life weren't on my radar anymore.

I got myself together, reminded myself of 100% expectation and 0% resistance, and did as I planned and set out on a little adventure. I got a cheap hotel room (much better than last time) and ended up taking a three-hour nap as soon as I got there! Guess I needed it!

When I awoke, the only thing I wanted to do was go back with my wife and family! I loved and missed them so much! But it would just have been silly to go away, just to come back home, so I pushed those thoughts aside. But I still had to facetime my wife for an hour, because I was missing her so much!

I found myself just flowing along different mental paths, which led to listening to music and songs that I had never heard before. I found some so very meaningful as they seemed to be exactly what I needed to hear!

Then, I found myself motivated to work and decided to start writing this book! I wrote the first two hours of it!!! Hurray!! Somehow writing this book was the solution! At the time, I didn't know it! I had no idea just how close I was to getting turned back on again!

Then, I just couldn't sleep all night and decided to come home at 6:00 AM the next morning! I think I was just so excited and balanced, unlike I had been in weeks!

Day 53

I had the bright idea of calling my insurance agent to see if, perhaps by some chance, any insurance coverage I might have would cover lost sales for this reason. Unfortunately, the answer was "no." But, being the awesome and loving person he is, he promised to pray for me, which deeply moved me. I truly felt his love and it was so meaningful.

I then spoke with another trusted business confidant, who helped me understand just how dire this situation was becoming. He encouraged me to start preparing for the worst, and helped me devise a multi-pointed plan of action, including personal, financial, inventory, warehouse, employees, and long-term perspectives.

One action item included trying to sell the inventory I had here to other local online sellers, in hopes of raising enough cash to pay the bills which were looming so ominously. So, I sent some emails and hoped for the best. I spent the rest of the day accomplishing many of the action items we had devised that morning. One of them included calling a realtor to assess my house value, with plans of selling it quickly to produce some much-needed short-term cash. This really hurt, but I did it.

LESSON 91: THE BEST WAY TO FEEL BETTER IS TO DO SOMETHING ABOUT IT. TAKE ACTION. ANY ACTION!

I realized today that I had spent a lot of time trying to deal with all my extreme emotions from this situation in so many ways. Many worked and helped me get through the days. But, none of them were actually moving me toward resolution; they were just helping me feel better and get through the days. My meetings today gave me the real action items I was so deeply craving. I just didn't know what to do and had no idea how to proceed, and every avenue was fraught with treacherous risks so great that I dared not go down any path!

Even though many of the action items I did today

were deeply painful, like the idea of losing my house and business, I still did them and deep inside I knew that I was moving forward. I was surprised at just how much better I felt, much better than all the self-soothing I had done before. This was because I *knew* these were appropriate and meaningful actions, which came from a trusted advisor who understood this type of situation.

As I went to bed tonight, I resolved to give up on any fight I might still be fighting with my marketplace facilitator. Truly, there was no fight and it had been over for nearly eight weeks already. Any fight that remained was only living in my mind, so I decided to let it die!

Day 54

I listened to a motivational YouTube video this morning, which spoke of how great the feeling of "on-the-verge-ness" was!

I spoke with some long-time friends, whom I had helped get into the e-commerce business ten years ago, and who promised to look over my inventory list and do what they could to help. This was so meaningful, because I knew they weren't in much of a position to do so, but they still promised to try!

I then spoke with my brother and sister-in-law, who were so good to us! They strongly assured us that we would not end up homeless, which was a deep, looming fear hiding just behind my consciousness all this time. That felt so good! They also made several other terrific recommendations including trying to sell on other marketplaces and hiring a consultant who specialized in this type of situation. Wow, what great advice! After hearing it, it seems so obvious, but somehow I had blinded myself to it all this time!

LESSON 92: A WELL-NEEDED EXPERT IS NOT AN EXPENSE, BUT AN INVESTMENT.

T wice so far, I had come across the same consulting firm who specialized in these types of situations, so I decided to look for them again. I found them easily and called. They answered and within 30 minutes I had used the last little bit of credit on one of my credit cards as well as one of my employees (have I mentioned the awesome team of employees I have!?!) to hire them. They said that within 24 hours they would have the ball rolling.

In the past, I would never have paid what they were charging, but somehow this just felt right and I knew there was little I could now lose. Either we were going to get turned on and somehow get out of this mess or I was about to lose everything I had spent the past 21 years building.

I learned that day to never see the cost of an expert

as an expense. Instead, see it as an investment, one that will pay dividends for months, years, and decades to come!

I then continued writing this book, completing the first 19 lessons! Afterwards, I spent some quality time with my son, which he desperately needed as I had been so consumed with this bump for nearly eight weeks now. Then I got an alternative marketplace account setup and they even approved me for an immediate seller-limit increase! Everything was flowing so well!

LESSON 93: NEVER DELEGATE TO OTHERS THAT WHICH ONLY YOU CAN OR SHOULD DO.

I n addition to trusting well-respected experts to bring incredible value, I also learned that it is important to not over-delegate. As I was digging deeper and deeper into my business, I saw that I had delegated many things to my employees which were things that only I could have done, or were things I truly should have been doing.

In this mistake, I not only missed the opportunity to see things from the unique and critical point of view that only an owner can see, but I suspect that I wrongly over-burdened my employees with challenges at which they simply weren't equipped to succeed.

I am not a lazy person, so I wasn't trying to get out

of doing things. It's that my logical mind keeps adding more and more to that which our business does, and as such, needs people who can do more and more of those tasks. What I failed to do was to take the time to properly assess what item I should be doing, especially for the reason of giving me insight into the health of the business in order to make proper high-level decisions.

Day 55

It seemed like everything was just flowing well today! I had a wonderful visit with a family member I hadn't seen for some time! Then, my Dad sent a truly motivational email, which, unknown to him, contained the exact lyrics of the song, "Every Little Thing (is going to be alright)" by Bob Marley, which had just been playing on my Alexa Shuffle!

It was one week before Christmas and I was feeling so grateful for having a full belly, a warm bed, a dry house, and a loving family. I truly had all I needed and that was enough. Everything else was just "fluff!"

I woke up at 3:00 AM with a sever terror attack! I couldn't see how I was going to survive. I knew things were looking good, but the terror had taken over my whole body and mind! I reminded myself that the negative I was feeling was simply an indicator that whatever was happening wasn't really in my best interest. I decided to try to replace the thoughts.

I tried... *hard* but it didn't work. I put on some motivational YouTube videos and meditations, for hours, but I just couldn't even hear them!

So, I played guitar for several hours and ended up feeling better. I was so glad to have had my friend, the guitar! I wrote some dark lyrics, which somehow helped me. I concluded that even though they were a strong negative expression of what I was feeling, they helped because I was *creating* something! I was making something actual out of potential, and this felt wonderful!

Somehow, as the sun was coming up, I was led to some other motivational YouTube videos, one of which resonated so deeply with me that I cried! I felt hopeful again!

Day 56

Today was sort of like the last day of class, where the teacher summarizes all the lessons taught during the semester, before the final exam.

Last night's meditation reminded me of a previous lesson about doing all I can each day, then resting. Somehow this sunk in, in a different way than before. It actually became a sort of battle-cry, which my subconscious mind kept repeating to me over, and over, and over, all day long!

A student gave a $100 gift card as a holiday gift -

this meant the world to me, because it was going to be so incredibly useful! I was reminded that where I am is good, and where I'm going is good, too! The Enya song, "Dreams are more precious than gold" played on Alexa Shuffle and its lyrics reminded me of just how critical my mental state is in all of this, so much more important than any money (gold) or lack thereof.

I was reminded that my active work is to keep a strong, focused mind. Only by doing so would I be able to move myself forward in the direction of my goals and dreams. I have been spending ten or more hours a day, seven days a week, for weeks now, over-hauling and redesigning many areas of our internal systems, so that when we're turned back on we can hit the ground running hard!

LESSON 94: YOU HAVE SURVIVED 100% OF YOUR PAST OBSTACLES.

I reminded myself that in the past I have overcome ALL obstacles that have come my way, in wonderful ways. Not a single obstacle has ever kept me down. This would be no exception! It is all about going through the day doing all the things I do to move forward, while faithfully believing they are bringing to me that which I desire!

This faith in receiving not only implies, but necessitates, that there be a source from which anything received must come. As I am learning these lessons, I am starting to see clearly that this source exists outside of myself, in its own sovereignty, and through its own intelligence. Some may call it God, the Universe, the Source, an Inner- Self, a Spirit Guide, your Guardian Angel, the Force, a Universal Power, the Life Force, an Indomitable Spirit, or many, many other names.

Regardless of its name, I am grateful for its infinite good, all the good it has brought me, and all the good it continues to offer everyone! I see more clearly now than ever that all I ever had to do was allow it, which is an underlying theme of most of the lessons in this book. After all, the infinite source of everything is effectively nothing to someone who won't allow it in.

LESSON 95: HAVING GONE THROUGH HELL WILL HELP YOU RELATE TO OTHERS WHO ARE GOING THROUGH HELL.

T his lesson sounds simple, but you just never know who, in your future, is going to need you to help them get through their hell. Only by having gone through your hell will you be able to help them.

I made a decision today: I am going to fight!!! I am not giving up!!! I am not giving in!!! I am going to get through this hell!!! I am going to shine brighter than I have ever shined before!! I am doing it for me, my family, and my employees! I am doing it for everyone!

I've got to get it done!!!!

This was big! From this moment on, there was no looking back.

I realized that the Fifth Tenet of Taekwondo is "Indomitable Spirit" which literally means someone can try to put your flame out 100 times and you'll relight it 101 times and carry on. I knew that I had indomitable spirit, now!

I had some sort of surrender inside myself. As mentioned in previous lessons, I gave up. I let go. I had a vision of living somewhere else, which was ok. I was playing my guitar and all my stress was gone! It was wonderful! I accepted, in that moment, that if losing everything I had cherished was the path I was on, then I was going to embrace that path, also. I could live a calm, creative life. I could teach Taekwondo. In fact, it wouldn't be any different than the past 5 years, financially, but with a lot less stress! I felt some sort of surrender to reality, to truth, to the universe, to whatever was about to happen.

By accepting this possibility, I realized what wouldn't change. My love for my family would not change. My love for my Taekwondo students wouldn't change.

I concluded: I will do all I can possibly do to survive this bump, while accepting that there is only so much I *can* do to affect the outcome.

As I fell asleep, I repeated over and over: "It's going

to be ok. I'm so close, now. I will get through. Yes, I will!"

LESSON 96: DOING YOUR BEST IS TRULY ALL YOU CAN EVER DO.

D ay 57

I have tried my absolute best. I truly am doing all I can possibly do. This wasn't me just making myself feel good by telling myself I was doing my best. I truly had done everything I possibly could have done.

I got together with another dear family member, whom I also hadn't seen for some time, and had beautiful, wonderful, loving time together.

Day 58

I woke up and happened to check my phone and saw sales! *WHAT?!?!?! SALES!??!!!!!??!! HOW COULD THAT BE??!!??!*

It turns out that we had gotten turned back on *yesterday* at 12:51PM! I didn't even know it! I had so completely surrendered to the universe and all it held, that I had no idea we had been turned back on!!! And what a wonderful sales day we had!

LESSON 97:
TEACH YOUR SUBCONSCIOUS MIND THAT YOU HAVE PLENTY... AND SOME TO SPARE!

I tried to see what I was doing at that moment, and traced my steps to having been giving special soups, which my Taekwondo Grandmaster had once given to me, to my mother who was ill with the flu! Somehow in my act of helping someone else, a good thing came to me.

I have concluded that generosity is what ultimately turned us back on. Of course the numerous changes I made resulting from all these lessons created the momentum which was moving us in the right direction. But by not entertaining feelings of competition, greed, or not having enough, my mind was able to accept the amazing blessings where were always abounding! I truly believe that the ultimate turning point was when my subconscious mind actually accepted, believed and felt that we have plenty, and even so much more than enough that I could share it with those we care for.

Take some time to exercise this concept into your subconscious mind. I changed my phone's opening screen to a message indicating this, which caused me to pause for just a moment each time I used my phone (100s of times a day). Then I forced myself to take the time to read it and allow the feeling to penetrate my whole self, each time. I estimate that I did this 500+ times before it really started to feel normal and I wasn't able to send any resistance to this idea whatsoever.

I also realized that we were turned back on *exactly eight weeks to the HOUR* from when we were turned off! Just incredible!

I *KNEW* I had to finish this book. I had to share this story and all its lessons with you, with the most sincere desire of helping someone else get through and out of any type of hard, horrible, disastrous, or seemingly impossible situation they may be going through... YOU might be going through.

I can see clearly how all this gave me perspective to get through the next year, as hard as I knew it would be. *I will never, ever again feel down about any situation!*

I realized I had such a wonderful time yesterday, without any regard one way or the other about whether we were still turned off or had been turned back on.

To my deep surprise, I wasn't nearly as happy now as I thought I would be about being turned back on again! But I quickly realized this is a good thing, because I was so happy already! I have been so joyful doing such good work.

Interestingly, today is the shortest day of the year. It all gets brighter from here!

Somehow, getting turned on and not even noticing it was exactly how it had to happen!

Final Lessons

Interestingly, the day after we got turned back on, I came down with the worst flu I've had in 20 years! And I rarely ever get sick! I guess it's just teaching me to take care of myself again, and also an indicator of just how far out of alignment I let myself go! Getting sick was a message for me to line up with my own energy and care for myself again!

Having skipped Christmas entirely this year, my Mom brought by a little Christmas tree and some beautiful decorations for it. How special, to feel loved in this way!

I found myself crying randomly. I guess this is another sign of stress relief from all I had gone through.

I continued to focus on the details of the business and ended up spending 80+ hours rewriting a whole bunch of our pricing and order fulfillment software, which was really essential to keep things flowing well, since so much had changed since I originally wrote it 5 years ago!

I knew I had "become one" with the flow, when I found myself waking up so many times at night with ideas of things I could do to improve the business even more! It felt like I was alive again, more so than I had been in 5+ years! This was wonderful!!

LESSON 98: IT'S FUN MAKING MONEY!

Whether or not you would have agreed with this statement at any time in your past, try allowing it in right now. Whatever you do to make money, find the fun elements of it! Make it a game! Make it a dance! Make it a party! Make whatever you do to make money super-fun! Teach your subconscious mind that this is true, by repeating it over and over all day!

I had been playing this mantra in my mind for weeks now and it really worked. I truly, finally, believed how fun it was making money! It was exciting to think of ways I could improve the business, things I could add, changes I could make, and how exciting it would feel when the first debt is paid, then the second, third, and on and on! Then one day, the debt will be all gone and maybe I'll get a nice boat or a vacation home in Florida! Or maybe the new 2020 Mid-Engine C8 Corvette!! It's FUN making money!! Make making money your personal adventure!

So, I assumed now that great sales were coming in, I'd see some money soon, to start paying all the bills that had racked up... NO! My largest short-term loan was actually from this marketplace facilitator, and they insisted on getting their back-payments, with interest, for the entire eight weeks we were down. Their minimum payment was so high that it took me *another* four weeks just to pay that down, which, of course, meant no income for a total of twelve weeks! I eventually did pay it back and *finally* the money started flowing!

At that time, I didn't even worry! In the past, this would have been devastating, but compared to what I had just been through, it was easy!

I think my ease regarding it allowed something wonderful to happen. When they contacted me and said I did, indeed, need to pay back all those payments, they happened to hint that perhaps I could refinance the remaining balance over a longer period of time. So, I asked and they gladly agreed, and even kept my interest rate the same! This will free up much-needed cash flow to allow me to purchase new inventory immediately, which will keep sales flowing and allow me to reach my goals!

I figure it will take about four months for me to fully dig out of what missing this holiday season cost me, but that will let me get a great start for the next year's season! (notice my genuine optimism again! It feels great!)

LESSON 99: YOU CAN'T PROPERLY UNDERSTAND THE TRUTH IF YOU'RE ANXIOUS.

When I was worrying and anxious about the future, I was tainting my current reality with fear and thoughts of failure. By doing so, I entirely missed so many opportunities. When I finally allowed happiness, joy, and excitement to replace my fear, sadness, and anxiety, everything improved.

Looking back, I can see how many times I really misinterpreted the situation itself, things that had happened, and people who were involved. The next time I feel anxious, I'll do my best to catch it early and remind myself that I won't be seeing things clearly as long as my mind is in that state.

Except for Christmas day, which I intentionally took off, I have been working twelve hours a day for weeks now and it feels *great!* As I mentioned in a previous lesson, take action, any action! As you move forward, you'll sense the changes in direction you'll want to make for the best outcomes. But you can only do this if you're moving forward. From a stand-still, nothing looks better or worse than anything else because you don't have any movement to compare points with each other!

LESSON 100: DESIRE + EXPECTATION = MANIFESTATION. GREAT DESIRE + GREAT EXPECTATION = GREAT MANIFESTATION.

I think this was the underlying lesson this whole time, which I could only understand from having been through this hell and coming back out of it. I think I had convinced myself that I had all the desire I needed, because I hated the situation I was in. But that wasn't true! I really had to work on my desire.

I knew I didn't want to be in this situation and that was a good start, but that was still focusing on the problem, not the desire for improvement. Only when I finally got my mind to *consistently*, without any wobble back and forth, *see and feel* the outcome I desired in a clear, calm, and focused manner, was I able to start working on the second part of this lesson... expectation.

Expectation was much harder than desire for me, because it seemed entirely impossible to expect something different from what all my logic and reason knew was the current situation. But little by little, I could feel my expectation shifting. At first, it was little elements of the situation which I could feel myself expecting, almost knowing, were going to improve. As several little ones shifted, I could feel slightly larger beliefs sliding over to the "we got this" side of the table from the "no way, man" side! Little by little, more and more, my mind expected a positive outcome from this whole situation.

All the past lessons led my mind to believe that I could *reasonably* expect a fruitful outcome, one way or another. In fact, it helped a lot for me to free my mind from *how* it was going to happen, and just trust, expect, and *know*, that a good and meaningful outcome was coming. I expected my desires to be fulfilled, and they were!

Looking back, I can see that *nothing* was going to change until I could *FULLY* desire the outcome

I wanted and expect it, seeing and believing it as though it had happened already. It wasn't just imagining. At first it was, but then as I practiced this concept more and more, it was as though I *knew* it already, just like I know I am sitting here typing on this computer right now. When there was no doubt at all, things started to shift and flow, faster and in more unique ways than I could have ever dreamed! But I had to do the hard job of really working my mind over and over and over into deeply knowing the outcome was nearly here, just as much as I know I am sitting here in my chair now.

LESSON 101: DON'T PUSH IT, DON'T PULL IT, AND DON'T FIGHT IT. ALLOW IT AND GO WITH THE FLOW.

T hroughout this book, I have mentioned the "flow" numerous times. This flow is the special life-energy which fuels our every action, every moment of our life. Think of all the things you learned in school that were necessary for life: Primarily food, water, air, clothing, shelter, and relationships. Now, imagine a dead person. Try giving him any or all of these things. They won't bring him back to life. That something-else which keeps us living is the life-force, or flow, which I am referring to in this book.

If you resist the flow, you are literally fighting with

life itself. The outcome is, obviously, all things syn-
onymous with lack-of-life, including sadness, poor
heath, meaningless work, inharmonious relationships, and even death itself. I learned so clearly
through both surviving this bump and writing this
book, that going with the flow is the *only* way to
thrive, which is another word for living abundantly,
joyfully, and healthily!

WHAT NOW?

Perhaps most surprising to me, looking back at this entire experience, is just how much more this entire episode turned out to be. In fact, this is the reason I changed this book's title from "Bump" to "Bounce". Bump implied that I had simply made it over an obstacle. Bounce so clearly illustrates how this seemingly negative event actually propelled me to greater heights than I ever could have expected!

So much of just *who* I am and *what* I value became clear through this experience. Many times, in these days since the "bounce," I have found myself dealing easily with things which might have distressed me prior to it. Things which would have seemed big are just small now! I find myself worrying less, smiling more, not caring about what others might think of me, and confidently moving forward with my life!

My relationships with *everyone* I care about have improved too. I find myself much less judgmental and more accepting of just who each person truly is. I find myself reflecting after each interaction about the numerous ways each person is inherently good and all the ways that just being who they are is perfect. I don't worry if someone hurts me, because I know they didn't mean it and I feel practically no pain from anyone's behavior anymore.

I can see myself more clearly now, too. I am so proud to be *me*! Sure, I strive to be better every day, in every way, but I am approaching it with a "go with it" attitude now, rather than "let me fix what is wrong with me!" What a big shift and magnificent feeling!

All through this situation, my heart kept telling me what was important. Now, I am listening to it. I find it easy to put my computer aside to spend 5 minutes with my son to help him practice saying the letters of his name or just dancing around the living room together. I guess what I'm saying is that by going through such an extreme low I now have ample perspective on that which matters in life, and am now able to also act from that perspective.

I find myself wishing that somehow I could have learned all this another way. Maybe I could have, if I had read a book like this. Or, perhaps, the only way would have been for me to have actually gone through it. My most sincere hope is that by reading this book, you are able to benefit from what I went through and perhaps avoid wasted time, energy, sadness, and expense, arriving at an equally wonderful place as I have now!

I hope that in reading this book, something inside you has shifted. Maybe, in some little (or big) way, you are different. Maybe you see the world differently. Perhaps your outlook on whatever your life is bringing you has swung in a new direction. Perhaps you've tried applying some of these lessons in your life already and experienced benefit from them. I sincerely hope that this book has propelled you in the direction of your dreams and helped you to remove unnecessary impediments from your mind.

I am so happy to be happy! Nothing is as bad as it seems! The world is full of amazing goodness! People are good! The world is great! There is more than enough money! Everything is working out perfectly! Good luck is abounding! Beauty is everywhere! And, there is *always* time for a hug! ALWAYS!

Now... Please go find someone you haven't hugged today, and hug them! Call someone you haven't spoken with in a while and let them know they matter to you. Find some way you have been out of balance with *yourself*, and correct it -- bring yourself back in to alignment and harmony. Right this moment, please give yourself exactly that which you need most!

The future is bright and life is wonderful! Now go live it!

About The Author

Ken Reiss is a seasoned entrepreneur, having started several successful businesses over the past three decades. He has always been an entrepreneur, even having sold plants as a child and floppy discs door-to-door to businesses, while in high school. His business career includes retail sales management and Internet development, both technical and marketing. He is also a software engineer, martial arts instructor, caring husband, and father to five wonderful children.

He can be reached at www.BounceLifeLessons.com.